T0110151

Redeemed

BEAUTY FROM DUST, RESTORATION FROM BROKENNESS, LIVING A LIFE REDEEMED

BELLE PRAF

WESTBOW
P R E S S®
A DIVISION OF THOMAS NELSON
& ZONDERVAN

WestBow Press books may be ordered through booksellers or by contacting:

WestBow Press
A Division of Thomas Nelson & Zondervan
1663 Liberty Drive
Bloomington, IN 47403
www.westbowpress.com
1 (866) 928-1240

Scripture quotations taken from The Holy Bible, New International Version® NIV® Copyright © 1973 1978 1984 2011 by Biblica, Inc. TM. Used by permission. All rights reserved worldwide.

ISBN: 978-1-9736-9680-3 (sc)
ISBN: 978-1-9736-9681-0 (hc)
ISBN: 978-1-9736-9679-7 (e)

Library of Congress Control Number: 2020912976

Print information available on the last page.

WestBow Press rev. date: 07/23/2020

Dedicated to my husband who has lived this with me, to family and friends that loved me at all times, to the ones who constantly point me to Jesus, and to the little ones who call me "Mommy."

Foreword

Belle Praf. It's not my name, but a name I'm writing under because this story isn't about me. This is not about my husband. This is not about our family. This is not about the devil or our small town. This is not about cheaters or broken marriages. This is not about churches or our friends. This book is not about us.

These words are about Him; His forgiveness, mercy, and protection amidst brokenness and sin. This story is about Him; His selfless love, provision, and peace in the darkest storm. This story is about a tireless victor, who never gave up, a God who cares and works all things together for our good. This story is about sinners in a dead world, running towards our only Savior, a situation deprived of light, now shining in His glory. This story is about a battle, fought and won by a King.

Belle meaning beautiful and Praf the Romanian word for dust because these words were written to show how, with God, beauty can and will come from the dust, His Kingdom brought glory from your most broken pieces.

I have sat down to write the words in these pages many times over the last couple of years. Some words were written through tear soaked eyes, some words were written in times of joy, and some words were written in months of devastation. But all of the words in this book you hold, were written specifically for you, for me, for anyone going through seasons of soul shattering.

Wherever you are in life or your walk with God, my prayer is that you will find Jesus here, in the midst of heartache and reconciliation. There is power in this story; I know because I have lived it, and I have seen Him move. I have seen Him bring beauty from the most shattered circumstances. I have seen Him make whole the finest pieces of dust, and the finished artwork is nothing like I pictured, like I planned, but it is beautiful, glory-filled, faith promised. You see, God brought me out of the darkness and into light, and through sin and struggles, I grew closer to Him, learned to rely on Him, learned to find fulfillment in Him alone, and that is a love story worth sharing.

I don't know what is broken for you right now, whether it's a relationship, an unfulfilled plan, a promise un-kept, but I do know that, whatever your circumstance, He is working. Whether you feel His presence or see His hand, His promise will be unbroken, and His plans for you are good.

I'm sharing these words, this testimony, with you, friend to friend, woman to woman, mom to mom because they are life changing. If we were sitting together, drinking coffee, there would be tears because this life is hard and full of heartache, but I would also tell you there is and there will be JOY. As women, we feel the need to be perfectly put together, but that is exhausting and impossible for us to do on our own.

The fact that you are holding this book, reading these words, hearing the testimony of a loving Savior, a merciful God, is proof that Jesus wins. His is the victory; I proclaim that truth over my life and yours. It doesn't matter what you have done in the past; it doesn't matter how broken and shattered your life is; it doesn't matter the sins you are drowning in. He came for you, and He came for me, and He didn't come expecting perfection, but right in the midst of our brokenness, He chose us to be REDEEMED.

Contents

Chapter 1   Dust 1
Chapter 2   Redeemed 11
Chapter 3   Prayer 19
Chapter 4   Lies 29
Chapter 5   Battles 39
Chapter 6   Trust 47
Chapter 7   Forgiveness 55
Chapter 8   Audience of One 65
Chapter 9   Fellowship 77
Chapter 10   Living in The Now 89
Chapter 11   "I am" 99
Chapter 12   Testimony 111

One

Dust

Surely, at some point in your life, you have been wrecked with the grief that comes with a disappointment. Disappointments can vary in magnitude, but they always leave a wake of devastation to the life you planned, the life you imagined. At my lowest, I felt like my entire world was crushed, shattered, debris of dust left from the flames of sin.

Did you picture yourself going on dream vacations? Having a well-paying and enjoyable job? Now, you're struggling with student loans and bills, and your job is less than fulfilling, or the work environment is draining joy from your soul.

Maybe you imagined white picket fences, a home filled with well-behaved children, or the "perfect" husband who washed dishes and completed every Pinterest project you found without complaint. Now, it hits you, and you realize that the fence posts are broken and chipped, your womb barren or empty, and your husband is falling short or maybe unfaithful. I don't know what your situation is. I don't know the life you planned or the heartaches you have faced, but I do know that

■ ■ ■

nothing is too shattered for Jesus.

■ ■ ■

In my research for this chapter, I found that there are 102 verses in the Bible that use the word "dust." The first mention is in Genesis when "the Lord formed a man from the dust of the ground and breathed into his nostrils the breath of life, and the man became a living being" (Genesis 2:7, NIV). I've heard this verse so many times, but I have never thought about why God chose to make the first living being, the first man made in His image, from the dust of the ground.

In my mind, He could have simply thought a man into being, and poof— there's Adam. After-all, He spoke and there was light, water, land, vegetation, the sun, and the moon. He simply spoke and there were creatures in the sea and birds in the sky and animals on the land.

But He didn't choose to speak man into existence. He chose to intricately and personally mold him out of the most unlikely of materials. He could have chosen something more sustainable, something more clean, something more glorious. But He didn't. He chose the dust from the ground.

■ ■ ■

This master Creator dirtied his hands to weave together the smallest broken pieces to make a living being.

■ ■ ■

It's more personal than saying for the sun to rise for day and the moon to rise for night. It's more personal than Him speaking a divide in the water and land. He chose to form us. He chose to form us and breathe life into our nostrils. He wanted to create us from dust, to use His hands, not just His voice, in the creation of His people, His workmanship.

■ ■ ■

We are a product of His hands.

■ ■ ■

Have you ever taken the time to make something? I often do crafts with our kids on rainy or cold days when we are stuck inside, and it always amazes me how much time and effort these toddlers put into their masterpieces. Their attention span is short with toys or books, but to put them in the role of a creator, to give them the ability to make something, their little tongues are out in concentration, and their little fingers are steady and purpose-filled, even with the most simple art of coloring or threading Fruit Loops on string. Then, when they are done, their eyes are bright, and you can see the joy that came with creating, and the happiness they feel to have made something from nothing.

Think then, how God spent time making you, molding you, forming you perfectly in His image and the goodness He has for you as your creator. We are His masterpiece. His love for us is shown in brightly painted sunsets. His glory shown in snow dusted peaks and crashing waves meeting sand. His intricate design and creativity are shown in our DNA, our faces, our eyes, our systems that work in sync and bodies that take years to study.

Have you doubted His ability to breathe life into the dust? Have you forgotten that He formed man from the dust of the ground? Have you lost sight of this master Creator who can mold beauty out of the most broken of pieces? What then, can He do with the dust of your life, if you choose to give it to Him?

There is pain in the letting go of what you think you deserve. There is fear in the unknown. There are cries of mourning over the ashes of a life you thought you would have, but those broken pieces, that dust, is exactly what God will remold into a masterpiece, a life healed and whole, and planned in love and understanding, specifically for you.

The dictionary definition of dust is a fine dry powder consisting of tiny particles of earth. Dust is a tiny, tiny particle, but from dust, comes clay, from clay, a sculpture or pot that has a purpose. It can hold water or maybe a planted flower.

■ ■ ■

Beauty can come from dust, depending on the potter.

■ ■ ■

Just as a potter creates a pot from clay, so God is working with us, taking the tiny pieces of dust, forming it, accepting and loving us as we are, and shaping us to His likeness- to His desire- for His purpose, something beautiful from ashes- from dust.

When my life was nothing but dust, I found that the only way I could look was up, to Him. Look up to the One who had been calling out all along, to the hushed voice, the love that never left. Look up to the only One able to breathe life into dust. In my brokenness, I found Him, and if I could rewrite my story, I would have found Him sooner, before my sin and mistakes because He was always there. But that very place of brokenness, the end of myself and the realization of my desperate need for a Savior, was the start of my deepest relationship with God. I fully trust God to make something beautiful out of the ashes, a trust and hope that could have only formed at my rock bottom.

I gave Him my broken pieces. I gave Him the pieces of my

marriage and relationships and life, so broken. I laid them at the feet of Jesus because no matter how hard I tried to sculpt something out of the dust; it only ran through my fingers. My hands were tired, and my abilities too weak because

■ ■ ■

we were not made to be the sculptor; we were made by the Sculptor.

■ ■ ■

Are you trying to fix something? Someone? A relationship? A financial situation? Please, please, listen to someone who tried and tried until my hands were raw from the clay that would not form; you cannot do it. If you are feeling broken, disappointed, staring at the dust of a situation surrounding you, give it to the God who chose to illustrate, from the beginning, His willingness and ability to breathe life into dust.

I want to show you His promise of goodness; His promise of beauty for ash. Read this excerpt from Isaiah 61.

"The Spirit of the Sovereign Lord is on me, because the Lord has anointed me to proclaim good news to the poor. He has sent me to bind up the brokenhearted, to proclaim freedom for the captives and release from darkness for the prisoners, to proclaim the year of the Lord's favor and the day of vengeance of our God, to comfort all who mourn, and provide for those who grieve in Zion— to bestow on them a crown of beauty instead of ashes, the oil of joy instead of mourning, and a garment of praise instead of a spirit of despair. They will be called oaks of righteousness, a planting of the Lord for the display of his splendor" (Isaiah 61:1-3, NIV).

Isaiah was a prophet who saw and wrote about the promises of God, and in this chapter, he was writing about the Year of the Lord's favor. This was a traditional year in Israeli society where the poor's

5

debts to the wealthy were wiped away. (Sign me up, right?! Ha!) But in all seriousness, I find so much peace in these words. Aren't we the poor, drowning in our own debt of brokenness and sin? And Jesus, with his life, wiped our debt free, not because we deserve it, but because He loves us.

Look at the language here: bringing good news, freedom for the captives, and the words joy instead of mourning. Doesn't that promise of praise instead of despair, and a crown of BEAUTY instead of ashes make you want to jump for joy? There is peace to be found in the God who promises these things.

He promises for us is to be called oaks of righteousness, planted to display His glory. And in the barrenness of desert land, to be large oaks was quite the promise.

■ ■ ■

The mourning won't last, and the prisoner will be set free because there is healing and comfort and joy in the name of Jesus.

■ ■ ■

I have debated what parts of my story to share with you, but my prayer has always been that God use my dust to restoration story for His good, His Kingdom. So, for you to fathom just how broken I was, my life, my marriage, my motherhood, my relationships, I'm going to share from a journal entry of the day my sin was brought to light.

"I will never forget the pain in my husband's eyes when he opened that door, the sound of his fist breaking through the drywall, the clatter of picture frames and spare change as it was strewn from the dresser, his shaky voice yelling, and the look of disgust and utter horror on his face as he loaded our kids and dogs in the car. I will never forget the confusion on our daughter's perfect little face as she questioned, 'Mommy's in trouble?'

I will never forget the words that came out of his mouth in shock and anger. How could he ever look at me again? Why would he ever want me again? His hurtful words went on and on.

I will never forget the numbness that took over my entire body. I was unable to fathom the hurt and pain that my actions caused, and I was disheartened by the fact that there was absolutely nothing I could do or say to fix it.

I felt so alone, sitting on the front porch of our dream home, where we talked of raising our kids and living our life together, but they weren't there anymore, my heart as empty as the rooms inside."

Can you feel the brokenness of a life shattered? I can still see the dust my life turned to in that moment. The holes left in our hearts, ragged and deep just like the hole left in the drywall. There was an overwhelming brokenness I didn't know we could ever repair. Shattered picture frames and spare change and drywall dust on the floor of our dream home, and my heart just hurt. There was fear and shame and despair in the illuminating of the darkness created by sin.

The only thing I could cling to in those first moments and the days after, was buried deep in my soul, pushed down by lies and sin, the knowledge of truth and forgiveness and God's ability to work ALL things out for our good. Even the most terrible sin-filled situation, can be made new when given to Him.

Since that day, I have endured seasons of reconciliation with my husband, seasons of his own betrayals, seasons of financial hardships, seasons of utter devastation, seasons of single parenting. But repeatedly, daily, moment by moment, I learned to bring my struggles to the only one capable of molding something beautiful from the dust in my life.

Learning to rely on Him as my Creator, my Potter, means that even when something I planned for, or hoped for, or prayed for didn't go according to my design, I trusted Him.

■ ■ ■

His promises of goodness and restoration are not based on my assumptions of what my life should look like.

■ ■ ■

Even when my marriage wasn't being reconciled, my relationship with Him was. Even when the restoration of my family didn't look like how I planned, even when healing didn't stick to my preferred timeline, I learned to trust the Potter with the sculpting.

I am the promised tall oak, a beaming beacon, a firmly planted reminder of how He can bind the broken hearted and pay off the debts of the poor, and I am the dust made clay formed into something new by His loving and capable hands.

Sweet friend, put down your tightly gripped dust, and let our Potter give you a crown of beauty. I promise that He will work in your life and do more good than you could ever dream of planning. Trade your brokenness for His wholeness. Let Him wash your debts away and find hope in the beauty to come because He is capable; He adores you, and we already know He is willing.

Reflection

o   What/who has disappointed you?

o   What is the "dust" in your life?

o   Have you given your brokenness to Jesus?

Prayer

God, you are the Creator of the Universe and the Creator of me. Your masterpieces are intricate and beautiful and wonderfully planned. Forgive me for my sin and the ways I try to control and scramble to fix my own brokenness. Thank you for your willingness and ability to mold my ash, my broken pieces into something beautiful, something new that will glorify you. Please take the dust of my life and create a finished product reflecting you and your goodness.

Two

Redeemed

Have you ever found yourself at rock bottom? Alone and scared and in trouble? Made choices and mistakes you regret? Have you ever shut God out? Maybe you haven't yet invited Him in. Have you ever muted His pleas for you to stop and come back to Him? Made selfish decisions? Made sinful decisions? Justified your actions all while spiraling into darkness? You are NOT alone.

Even writing those questions, I feel as if I need to raise my own hand, maybe both, shamefully saying, "Yes, I have." Satan wants you to feel alone; he wants to isolate you, make you feel unworthy and unloved, instead of the adored child of God that you are.

Our nature is to sin. We were made for perfection, relationship with God, but it was broken with a single bite of fruit. Ever since the Garden, when Eve decided our destiny and chose wisdom over perfect communion with God, people have chosen self over service, self over God's glory, self over spouse, self over everything and anyone else.

If I look in the mirror at my own soul, I want to control, and I want to do things that only make me happy, and I want to listen to the lies of Satan, and I want to scream because that is not the reflection of Christ in me. Even on my best days, where I chase after God and fill my soul with His Word, even when I cultivate my relationship with Him through prayer, I am not enough.

We are sinners in a fallen world, self-servers in nature, sin choosers at heart, wisdom stealers since the beginning. But God. How thankful I am for that "but." But God chose to love us anyway. So much so, that He made a way through blood and grace for us to come running back to Him- out of the Garden and into His arms, open wide. By His grace, we are saved; redeemed. "In Him we have redemption through His blood, the forgiveness of our sins, in accordance with the riches of God's grace that He lavished on us" (Ephesians 1:7-8, NIV). The same God, who chose to form and mold us from dust, chose to redeem our souls despite our sinful hearts. Through His blood, we are forgiven our trespasses; we are His chosen redeemed, and we are made rich by His free grace given.

The word redeemed has three common definitions or uses. One means to buy or purchase freedom, another to buy something for another purpose, and the third is purchasing off a debt. Think about this word; this lavish gift we have in redemption.

We are the slave bought free, slaves to sin purchased into freedom by the life of Jesus. We are the something bought for greater purpose. Souls condemned, made new; lives changed and purpose-filled, to bring His Kingdom glory. Ours is the sin, the debt wiped free. Do you feel that weight being lifted?

He knows my heart. The one reflected in the mirror full of hate and fear and resentment. He doesn't just shatter the image I see of myself; He completely replaces it with the perfect image of Christ. When you choose a relationship with Him, and believe that Christ died and rose, and that our sins were nailed to the cross with Him,

■ ■ ■

His blood covers every painful and shameful reflection of sin.

■ ■ ■

I believe this. I have believed this. But I have never felt the power of forgiveness until I was at rock bottom, a shadow of myself, crying out, feeling the weight of my sin and selfish mistakes. I felt like this sin would take more forgiving, more grace. I was at rock bottom, alone and questioning how I got there.

In the shadows, you feel alone, unwanted, ashamed. The light is always there, although faint when you are in the depths of shadows. You will never be happy or fulfilled in the darkness because you were created for light. And any of Satan's whispers saying you are unworthy, or you can be in control, or that you are too broken or unworthy, are lies. He says you're fine, not to worry, there is no brokenness here. But God is also with you in the darkness, His light casting the shadows because you are never too far to reach.

I have lived in the light and endured seasons of chosen darkness. In the shadows, I was an outline of myself, choosing sin and hurting people that I love. I cried out to God- I was so broken and so far from Him. I shut Him out, pushed Him away over and over, justified my sin, denied His help, even as He kept calling out to me. I realized the hurt that I caused, the wake of devastation caused by sin, and still I knew, He was there. My heart ached for His forgiveness, and my voice begged for it. In His light, I am still a sinner, but I am redeemed. I can love and serve because of His strength and the fulfillment that can only come through a relationship with Him.

If your soul is not reflecting Jesus, if you are surrounded by darkness, turn to Him. Admit your failures, acknowledge your inabilities, and learn to rely on His perfection and His ability. Get out of the shadows and step into the light of Jesus: vibrant with color and unimaginable warmth. There is truth and promise and goodness. You can fulfill your purpose and love unconditionally and serve unselfishly.

After repenting and receiving forgiveness from Jesus, you also have to forgive yourself.

■ ■ ■

Focusing on guilt and shame
hold us back from God's power
to allow us to start over.

■ ■ ■

If you are going to live a life redeemed, you have to believe that you are saved; believe you are who He says you are.

Church on Sunday isn't enough. Saying a blessing before a meal isn't enough. Occasionally opening your Bible isn't enough. If we don't cling to Him with all of our might, we are capable of terrible things, things that lead to broken marriages, broken families, and broken hearts, but He is persistent and forgiving, and He is the healer for all the brokenness.

There is a parable Jesus tells in Luke 15 to the tax collectors and sinners who were gathered to hear Him speak. The Pharisees were grumbling because they thought Jesus spent too much time with sinners, choosing to eat at their tables, and Jesus responded with this story.

"Suppose one of you has a hundred sheep and loses one of them. Doesn't he leave the ninety-nine in the open country and go after the lost sheep until he finds it? And when he finds it, he joyfully puts it on his shoulders and goes home. Then he calls his friends and neighbors together and says, 'Rejoice with me; I have found my lost sheep.' I tell you that in the same way there will be more rejoicing in heaven over one sinner who repents than over ninety-nine righteous persons who do not need to repent" (Luke 15:4-7, NIV).

In this parable, and so many others that Jesus told while he was on earth, we are the sheep. We are the stubborn, defenseless, prone to wander sheep. Sound about right? So if we're the lost sheep, Jesus is the shepherd, leaving the ninety-nine to find his one lost sheep. He leaves his ninety-nine other sheep, the ones that didn't run away, the ones that followed as they should, to find the one lost sheep. To find the one who did run, who did wander, who didn't listen, who thought he could do it on his own.

We are the soul found that He joyfully embraces and brings home to shout in rejoice with his neighbors and friends that YOU have arrived. We are the sinner repenting, the reason for rejoicing in heaven. We are the ones Jesus chose to spend his numbered days with despite the remarks and judgements from the "holy" religious leaders. He spent his time on earth choosing to sit at the table of sinners, loving and healing the broken with his own life.

This parable is a perfect representation of how Jesus cares for you. He redeemed you and me. He purchased us for something greater and payed our debt with his own life. And he didn't do it because we deserved it; he did it because he loves us.

By not confessing your sin and realizing your inability and brokenness, you are denying yourself the fulfillment of His good promises for you. You are denying yourself the greatest gift ever given. You are denying yourself a life, an eternity, redeemed.

How then, do we live a life reflecting redemption? It starts by accepting our brokenness and need for saving. Accept that the dark places of your heart are made bright by the blood of Jesus, and trust that His grace removes your shame.

Being a mom is the hardest thing I have ever been called to do. There are always diapers to change, laundry to do, floors to clean, hair to comb, dirty hands to wash, and it is so exhausting having patience amidst tantrums over the wrong color cup or screams over toys not being shared. Being a mom has humbled me because I cannot do it alone. I go daily to the Father with my hands up in surrender because my flesh gets angry and frustrated, but His ability gives me joy and grace, even on the hardest days of mothering.

This is how it should be in all aspects of our lives. Living a life redeemed is being able to praise Him in the storm and the rays of sun. Living a life redeemed is finding joy on the hardest days because this life is fleeting and our troubles here will be plenty, but

■ ■ ■

to live a life redeemed is to know that we are promised freedom and adoration and saving, even when we continuously fall short.

■ ■ ■

"Give thanks to the Lord, for he is good; his love endures forever. Let the redeemed of the Lord tell their story— those he redeemed from the hand of the foe, those he gathered from the lands, from east and west, from north and south.

Some wandered in desert wastelands, finding no way to a city where they could settle. They were hungry and thirsty, and their lives ebbed away. Then they cried out to the Lord in their trouble, and he delivered them from their distress. He led them by a straight way to a city where they could settle. Let them give thanks to the Lord for his unfailing love and his wonderful deeds for mankind, for he satisfies the thirsty and fills the hungry with good things.

Some sat in darkness, in utter darkness, prisoners suffering in iron chains, because they rebelled against God's commands and despised the plans of the Most High. So he subjected them to bitter labor; they stumbled, and there was no one to help. Then they cried to the Lord in their trouble, and he saved them from their distress. He brought them out of darkness, the utter darkness, and broke away their chains. Let them give thanks to the Lord for his unfailing love and his wonderful deeds for mankind, for he breaks down gates of bronze and cuts through bars of iron.

Some became fools through their rebellious ways and suffered affliction because of their iniquities. They loathed all food and drew near the gates of death. Then they cried to the Lord in their trouble, and he saved them from their distress. He sent out his word and healed them; he rescued them from the grave.

Let them give thanks to the Lord for his unfailing love and his wonderful deeds for mankind. Let them sacrifice thank offerings and tell of his works with songs of joy" (Psalms 107:1-22, NIV).

This Psalm speaks of my life. The foolish seasons of darkness and chains and cries out to God in desperation. Every wandered moment, forgiven by undeserved grace and mercy and a safe place given to settle. Every rebellious moment met with arms wide open, saving and need realized. Every dark moment spent wallowing made light and made new, so I will tell of His continuous rescuing. Let the redeemed of the Lord tell their story, speak of the ways He saved you over and over, this tireless victor, this unfailing love because before we even needed it, He was planning our redemption.

They wandered and grew hungry and thirsty. They rebelled and sat in chains, and they were bitter and suffered afflictions because of their choices. They drew near to death. And each time they chose to wander because we're stubborn, stubborn sheep. But, they cried to the Lord in their trouble. And he didn't say, "I told you so," or rub defeat in their face. Instead, He healed and provided and broke chains and rescued them from the grave. So, they praised Him.

God's ability to forgive is unfathomable. It's a free gift given, after asking and repenting, grace given when undeserved, mercy flowing when we continually choose the fruit. Over and over we deny Jesus and the freedom of the cross, insisting we can do it on our own, convincing ourselves that we don't need saving. But don't you just look up sometimes and realize you've wandered? How thankful I am in those moments to look up and see my Shepherd. No matter how far I run, He will find me, and He will find you too. Can you hear Him calling you back? His treasured sheep, stop wandering alone and on your own, and return to Him.

My life and decisions made apart from God have shown how desperately I need Jesus, and because He is merciful and loving, He forgives us. Living a life redeemed isn't perfection. It's the opposite.

It's knowing that you are incapable, but praising the One who is capable. He restores your soul, your relationship with Him, your identity in Him, your purpose for Him. Let your life reflect the utter need for redemption. Your failures only magnify His glory, and He is waiting, always, arms open.

Are you listening to the lies of Satan? Do you feel too guilty to be saved? Too in debt to pay? Too captive to break chains? Don't let the enemy or people tell you that you are anything less than the perfectly molded from dust, Spirit breathed-life, redeemed child of God that you are.

Reflection

o   What sins are you struggling with?

o   How can you live a life redeemed?

Prayer

Lord, you are my Savior. You are forgiving and grace filled, and your love is unconditional. I have been a lost sheep, needing the guidance from my Shepherd. Forgive me for wandering. Forgive me for the ways I continually fall short. Thank you for redemption. Thank you for joyfully welcoming me home. Thank you for arms wide open and celebration of a soul found. I pray that you will guide me, keep me close, and help me to live a life reflecting a heart redeemed.

Three

Prayer

Growing up in church, I remember praying. I remember my mom teaching me the "Now I lay me down to sleep" bedtime prayer and committing to memory the "Lord's Prayer," and we had a prayer we said before meals. As I grew up, the prayers of my childhood subsided and more of a conversation began. Mostly, I would pray to God asking for things: help with grades and tests, or a boy to like me, or prayers for my friends and family. Then, for jobs and marriage and kids and bills.

■ ■ ■

Our prayers evolve as our needs and dreams do.

■ ■ ■

As we get older and more mature, don't our prayers get more in depth? Our problems and hardships increase and hearts break and people get sick, and our prayers get louder, and our pleas are more frequent. Gone are the rhyming memorized verses, and in are the guttural cries for help.

My mom was diagnosed in her college years with Lupus. There were medicines to help her kidneys function and chemo to keep the flares at bay, but her body was affected by this disease and even by the medicines used to quiet the symptoms. Her active life was threatened by a heart attack and then paralysis when the disease moved to her Central Nervous System. There was fear in her hospital room as we waited for any feeling to return to her legs, there were tears of fear and the unknown, but there was also faith in the God we knew as Healer. For the first time in my "adult" life, I cried out to God.

I cried out, begging for His healing hand, but each day, her paralysis remained. Could He not hear me? Was I not praying enough? Was I not asking correctly? I knew He could heal her; I knew He was capable. I grew up reading the miraculous stories of Jesus. About the paralyzed friend who was lowered into the room and walked out the front door, but my prayers went unanswered. This was the first time I asked God for something big, something miraculous, and I grew angry when He didn't answer, when He didn't do what I asked of Him.

Do you have unanswered prayers? Are you feeling as if your words are bouncing off the sky? Prayer is our way of communicating with God, our adoration, confessions, thankfulness, and our needs. Prayer is not a time for us to enter our order into a vending machine and expect our item promptly.

■ ■ ■

In a world with Amazon Prime and same day delivery and fast food drive throughs, we have grown impatient with waiting.

■ ■ ■

"Rejoice in the Lord always. I will say it again: Rejoice! Let your gentleness be evident to all. The Lord is near. Do not be anxious about anything, but in every situation, by prayer and petition, with thanksgiving, present your requests to God. And the peace of God, which transcends all understanding, will guard your hearts and your minds in Christ Jesus" (Philippians 4:4-7, NIV). The Bible doesn't say to ask and you will get anything you want. It doesn't describe God as a vending machine that supplies your immediate wishes. These verses say to rejoice in who God is, to not be anxious, to pray in every situation, not just the difficult, and to present our requests to God. It doesn't say that God will answer in two days or two years, but it says that the PEACE of God, which surpasses all of our understanding, will guard our hearts.

He is a loving God who wants to hear your heart and desires, but He loves you enough to keep you safe from things that might hurt you. He is also all knowing, so His understanding of the world and the plan for our lives is the whole picture, where we only see our past and current situations.

■ ■ ■

By praying to God our praises, our hardships, our desires, we aren't promised to always get what we asked for, but we are promised His peace.

■ ■ ■

When my world was falling apart, I prayed. I prayed like my life depended on it because in so many ways it did. Some of my prayers were answered quickly, and I was in awe, but some weren't answered right away, and it was okay because I had that promised peace. In the middle of the hardest season of my life, I truly had peace. My life was falling apart, but I had an overwhelming peace that could have only come from relationship, from prayer, from communication with God. When you pray, you're sharing yourself, your life, your troubles, your joys with God, and that gives you utter peace in any circumstance.

What are you praying for in this season of your life? A broken marriage? A sick family member? A dream house? A better job? A child? Whatever it is, know that even when your prayers go unanswered, you are being heard by the King.

■ ■ ■

Let your faith in Him grow in your waiting, and know that His timing for you is perfect.

■ ■ ■

for you is perfect. Feel His peace wash over you, and know that He has good, good plans for you.

Let's look at a story of waiting and prayer from 1 Samuel. A story of Hannah and a barren womb and lessons learned in the waiting. Hannah's Husband, Elkanah, had two wives; Hannah and Penninah, and Penninah had children, but Hannah had none. Year after year her husband would make sacrifices, giving a double portion for Hannah because he loved her so, and because her womb was closed.

"Her husband Elkanah would say to her, 'Hannah, why are you weeping? Why don't you eat? Why are you downhearted? Don't I mean more to you than ten sons?' Once when they had finished eating and drinking in Shiloh, Hannah stood up. Now Eli the priest was sitting on his chair by the doorpost of the Lord's house. In her deep anguish Hannah prayed to the Lord, weeping bitterly. And she made a vow, saying, 'Lord Almighty, if you will only look on your servant's misery and remember me, and not forget your servant but give her a son, then I will give him to the Lord for all the days of his life, and no razor will ever be used on his head.'

As she kept on praying to the Lord, Eli observed her mouth. Hannah was praying in her heart, and her lips were moving but her voice was not heard. Eli thought she was drunk and said to her, 'How long are you going to stay drunk? Put away your wine.' 'Not so, my lord,' Hannah replied, 'I am a woman who is deeply troubled. I have not been drinking wine or beer; I was pouring out my soul to the Lord. Do not take your servant for a wicked woman; I have been praying here out of my great anguish and grief.' Eli answered, 'Go in peace, and may the God of Israel grant you what you have asked of him.' She said, 'May your servant find favor in your eyes.'

Then she went her way and ate something, and her face was no longer downcast. Early the next morning they arose and worshiped before the Lord and then went back to their home at Ramah. Elkanah made love to his wife Hannah, and the Lord remembered her. So in the course of time Hannah became pregnant and gave birth to a son. She named him Samuel, saying, 'Because I asked the Lord for him'" (1 Samuel 1:8-20, NIV).

So much of this story resonates with me. Broken hearted Hannah and her loving husband who blamed himself and questions why he isn't good enough for her. Doesn't she love him? Why does she need a child to be happy? The emptiness of her womb causing anguish, the quietness of her home heartbreaking, when all she wanted was a son's laughter to fill the rooms. Her heart ached to hear the footsteps. She felt this calling to motherhood, yet year after year, her womb and her nursery remained empty.

She went to the Lord in desperation, praying, weeping bitterly. She was angry, frustrated, for years she prayed and asked and tried to get pregnant. She begged God not to forget her, and she "kept on praying to the Lord" (1 Samuel 1:12, NIV). In her anguish, she made promises to God. Sarah bargains that if God gives her a son, she will never cut his hair. Have you been there? God, if you do this for me, I will stop ____: cussing, speeding, gossiping.

She prayed so fervently, lips moving, eyes closed, that her husband thought she was drunk. Surely, she's had a little too much wine, and that's what was causing this outburst. But these cries weren't caused by drunkenness. These were cries of desperation, guttural cries of a soul not whole, whispers to the One she knew could provide.

Hannah responds to her husband's accusations of drunkenness by saying she was troubled and praying out of her anguish and grief, not drunkenness. I know that prayer; I have prayed from that same place of frustration and brokenness. After she prayed, that sick feeling in her stomach released and she was able to eat, and her face was no longer downcast because

■ ■ ■

that pouring out of prayer, allowed God's peace to fill her up.

■ ■ ■

Early the next morning, she worships God. In these difficult seasons, isn't it easy to just pray and ask and look for answers? Do you forget to worship and praise God for what He has already done? Praise Him for who He is, who He has always been, and who He will remain to be despite the circumstances you are facing.

Look at the words chosen here, "so in the course of time Hannah became pregnant" (1 Samuel 1:20, NIV). Isn't it funny how it doesn't say the next month or the next year that she conceived a child? Nope; in the course of time; His time. What prayer do you want God to answer today, tomorrow? What circumstance do you want resolved now instead of His course of time?

Friend, I will tell you from experience that

■ ■ ■

there is power in prayer; there is peace in prayer, and there is reason for the waiting.

■ ■ ■

Over the last couple of years, I have prayed more than I have in my entire life. I have prayed for forgiveness; I have prayed for my marriage; I have prayed for basic necessities, like food and electricity. I have prayed for bills and financial problems; I have prayed for our children- their faith and futures. I have prayed in thanksgiving, praise to the God who loves and forgives and breaks chains. I have prayed for the ability to forgive myself and others. I have prayed for friends and relationships and loved ones diagnosed. I have fasted and prayed for life altering situations. And in all of my praying, I have seen immediate answers, words uttered and an unexpected check arrived in the mail, words whispered and a job acquired. But I have also seen "in His time" answers, words cried and cried and cried, never ceasing because I know He is the one to bring them to, and still, to this day, not seeing the answers. In my waiting, I have gained faith that can only come from reliance on Him, that peace that can only come from giving Him every aspect of your life.

Over and over, year after year, Hannah desperately and fervently asked God for a son. Think of the faith built in continuously trusting and knowing that God was the only one able to give that to her. I'm sure she had moments of doubt, fears of being infertile forever, and probably even chastisement for believing that God would give her a son in her old age after years and years of childlessness.

But the Lord remembered Hannah and gave her Samuel because she asked the Lord for him, not because of her righteous character, not because of her husband's sacrifices, but because she faithfully and fervently asked the Lord for him, Samuel was born. A man who was called by God, not once, but three times. A man who was a priest, judge, prophet, and military leader, raised by a mother whose faith and character grew through prayer and waiting.

Your prayers may seem unanswered, or they may be answered immediately, but in the course of time, His perfect all knowing time, goodness will come, whether it is what you asked for, or something entirely different, trust that it will be good.

My mom is still paralyzed, still immobilized by life in a wheelchair, but her faith remains. A faith I have seen despite the grieving that came with legs that no longer work. Despite the ways her active life has changed by being bound to a wheelchair. Despite the dreams shattered of scooping up grand children or running alongside their bikes or giving them piggy back rides. The faith that God is Healer, and knowing that He has used her faith in her circumstances to inspire others and build His Kingdom, is only a glimpse of His goodness.

The days and nights in that hospital long ago, praying and singing about Jesus' goodness in all circumstances, now foundational to my own faith. Nine years later, she still looks to God as her Healer. The Provider for her everyday needs, strength and energy and joy through her physical and emotional hardships. And if not in this life, the next, she will be running and leaping with joy in heaven, having lived a life trusting and growing in the waiting.

Let your faith in Him grow; keep believing that He is the one to bring your prayers to, and rest in the waiting with His promised peace.

■ ■ ■

Seasons of need and prayer and maturation and a learned reliance on God will prepare you for the goodness and answers in store.

■ ■ ■

Reflection

o   What prayers do you feel are unanswered?

o   How is your faith growing through prayer in your season of waiting?

Prayer

Jesus, you hear my prayers. You hurt with me; you know what is best for me; you have a good, good plan in store. Forgive me for thinking I know best. Forgive me for wanting answers when I want them. Thank you for always hearing and knowing and loving me. Take my prayers, my heart, my life, God, they're yours. Help me to trust your perfect timing. Help my faith in you grow in this season of waiting, knowing you hear me, knowing your plan for me is good.

Four

Lies

There are many lies we hear daily about who we are, or what our purpose is, or how religion is supposed to reflect in our lives. We hear lies about who we are supposed to be as moms, women, wives. Since the garden, Satan has quietly slithered into our hearts and lied and manipulated and sought to drive us away from God. He seeks destruction and death, and his lies will leave you in desperation and desolation.

"Be alert and of sober mind. Your enemy the devil prowls around like a roaring lion looking for someone to devour" (1 Peter 5:8, NIV). You need to be aware of him prowling, know the roar of his lies, so that you will not be devoured, but protected by truth.

Out of all the lies he tries to tell you, I'm going to focus on four that I struggle with the most, and then I'm going to cover that lie with the truth we know from God. The lies may come from friends or family or even your own mind, but if they aren't from the truth of God, they will only tear you down.

"To the Jews who had believed him, Jesus said, 'If you hold to my teaching, you are really my disciples. Then you will know the truth, and the truth will set you free'" (John 8:31-32, NIV). You will hear lies in your life. You will most certainly encounter them, but when you learn the truth, you will be free. You will be able to identify the lies and not let them steal your joy.

Lie #1: Fulfillment (You need more)

Have you ever felt like something or someone could make you feel better, more whole? Like, you would just be happy if _____ (fill in the blank). If my debt was paid off, if my home was decorated perfectly, if my kids behaved, if I had that purse or that outfit, if my husband showed his love more often, if my body was healed, I would be happy. There are so many earthly things that the enemy uses to tempt us, to make us feel like we could be more fulfilled.

■ ■ ■

The problem with relying on earthly things to bring us fulfillment is that people are imperfect, and jobs are unstable, and vacations are fleeting, and the joy that they bring doesn't last.

■ ■ ■

Have you ever been so looking forward to something? You know those feelings of anticipation and excitement? I still remember the butterflies I felt in the weeks, months leading up to our wedding. I can still feel the joy of waiting in lines for ice cream as a child. When we have exciting weekend plans, I countdown the days until Friday.

Our kids get so excited for Christmas. We spend days decorating and weeks enjoying the lights and songs that go along with the holiday. You can see the joy on their faces when the basement-stored

Christmas boxes come out, and they stay up late with anticipation on Christmas Eve, excitedly expecting their gifts they will receive the next morning. There is nothing wrong with the happiness that this gives them. God wants us to live lives full of happiness, but we need to make certain that these moments aren't what we are relying on completely for our fulfillment because Christmas ends and new toys become old toys and the decorations and lights are returned to their boxes, but the joy of Jesus' birth is year-round.

Do you see how joy brought by things on earth is fleeting? Seeking fulfillment from having many friends fails because friends move and friendships change, and seeking fulfillment from making the perfect dinner fails because your kids decided they don't like noodles now. Seeking fulfillment from your husband fails because he's tired, and his day was long. People perish or move away, circumstances change, but God remains and will never change.

Are you ready for the truth that covers this lie? This lie that anyone or anything on this earth will fulfill you? That something or someone could possibly sustain you?

Truth: Jesus is the Bread of Life

The truth that covers this lie of earthly fulfillment is that Jesus is the only thing that can ever fill us wholly, lastingly.

"Then Jesus declared, 'I am the bread of life. Whoever comes to me will never go hungry, and whoever believes in me will never be thirsty'" (John 6:35, NIV).

This verse in John, these words Jesus spoke, say that Jesus is the bread of life. Bread is a timeless food, still relevant and definitely eaten even 2000 years after he said this, and craved by dieting women everywhere. It's a filling comfort food, a pantry staple. Actual bread consumed gets ingested and digested, and then after, you are hungry again. But Jesus, as figurative bread, will never leave you hungry. Oh, and because he knew you would need something to wash it down, guess what? Believe in Him, and you won't be thirsty either.

■ ■ ■

Fullness and joy are not slaves to our circumstances, but they are free gifts from a God who loves in abundance.

■ ■ ■

He is the provider of edible bread and sustainer of spiritual bread, and when you believe in Him and live in relationship with Him, you will NEVER go hungry or thirsty. He can rain down Manna from Heaven or pour you a cup of Living Water, if you let Him, if you seek Him daily for the only wholeness that will ever fulfill you.

He is the bread we need to live. He provides the actual bread we eat, and He is the only bread that fills our souls. He is the bread that was broken to save us from sin, and the bread we should crave most.

Lie #2: Isolation (You are alone)

The second lie that I struggle with, especially as a mom and wife and woman is that I'm alone in my struggles. I stayed at home with our kids for years, and I have never been so surrounded by people who need me and talk constantly, but some days felt so utterly alone. As a wife, I listen to the lies of Satan telling me I'm the only one struggling to clean and do the dishes and still look cute for my husband, or have anything to talk about other than kid toys and who did what to the toilet paper, if we actually get a date night.

The lies say you can fix your circumstances yourself, or that no one understands, or that your sins are too great to confess. When you're in the darkness of these lies, you detach from friends or family or church because darkness flees light. You isolate yourself to deal with sin and lies and hardships on your own, ashamed, only to be dragged further down. These lies separate you from people who can speak truth into your circumstances, forcing your faith to stand alone when we were made for fellowship and testimony.

If Satan can isolate us, he can deceive us even further, and his lies start to sound like truth, and that is a scary place to be.

Truth: Immanuel, God With us

The truth is that we are never alone in our struggles, our storms, or even our triumphs. "'The virgin will conceive and give birth to a son, and they will call him Immanuel' (which means 'God with us')" (Matthew 1:23, NIV). From before Jesus' birth, the promise of his presence came with the name Immanuel. God with us. And the promise of his presence wasn't just with his numbered days on earth, but through the inviting in of His Spirit, all of our days. "But whoever is united with the Lord is one with him in spirit" (1 Corinthians 6:17, NIV).

In the Old Testament, the presence of God was most evident when His glory filled the tabernacle and the temple, but in the New Testament, God came in flesh, a baby born of this earth, God physically with us.

He isn't just watching and observing from Heaven; He isn't just at church or the holy places; He isn't only accessible to pastors or priests. He is WITH us; He is IN us, and that means that even when we feel alone, we aren't. That means that even when lies and sin creep in, He is there.

There is no hiding from Him. Acknowledge that He is with you always. Let the truth of His presence de-isolate your heart and find healing in fellowship with Him and others.

Lie # 3: You Aren't Loved

This lie is the hardest for me. If you haven't taken the Enneagram test to see what personality type you are, put down this book and google it! You will learn SO much about yourself and your relationships and your fears, strengths, and weaknesses.

Without getting all technical because I am no psychologist or personality expert, my test concluded that I am Type 2, The Helper. If you have no idea what that means, let me break it down for you. My personality seeks approval and acceptance of others, seeks to be a source of support and help in all relationships, and do you know what the greatest fear for this personality type is? To feel unloved.

Deep down, I want to love and support and feel that my acts of service are appreciated and acknowledged. When I didn't feel this in my marriage, it led to desperation and fear. I listened to the lies that I deserved more. I let the lies of Satan tell me that I needed adoration and praise. Friend, let me tell you, those lies led to a path of utter destruction. All because I felt unloved and unappreciated, and don't we just feel that from the people in our lives sometimes?

All the kitchen cleaning and toilet scrubbing and meals cooked and cards written and extra chocolate chips in the cookies go unnoticed, and when those feelings of resentment rise, we are capable of terrible things. If we don't bring those thoughts, those lies directly to the Father, who does love and does appreciate and does see every little act of love, our hearts will break.

Truth: Beloved, Child of God

When we feel unloved and unappreciated and unworthy in this life, and I hate to say it, but you will, we need to immediately check our hearts with God's truth. Listen to what He did for YOU because of His unconditional, unfathomable love:

"But God demonstrates his own love for us in this: While we were still sinners, Christ died for us" (Romans 5:8, NIV). Right in our sin and brokenness, He sent His son to die for us.

Do you have children? Can you imagine giving your own child to save people whose hearts are dark, who wander, who by nature choose to do wrong, who daily lie and steal? But, what if those you were saving were also your children, who you love just as much, even with their imperfections. Isn't that unconditional love? God is defined over and over by His love, and we as His people can then be identified in Him by our love for others.

Don't ever let the feelings or thoughts of anyone on this earth make you feel anything less than His child, His beloved, His chosen people to be redeemed by the blood of His son. Talk to Him daily. Spend time reading His truth because knowing who you are in Him, how loved you are by Him, is exactly what your soul needs to feel truly loved.

Lie # 4: Fear (You should be afraid)

This life is full of things to fear. I'm afraid of heights, roller coasters, health issues, snakes, relationship problems, spiders, bills and debt, my kids' faith and futures, rodents of any kind, relinquishing control, and I really could go on and on. What scares you?

When you are afraid, your body responds physically; your breathing and heart rate increase, some of your blood vessels constrict, and some of your blood vessels dilate to flood your organs with oxygen, and your muscles are pumped full with blood. Goosebumps, blood sugar, adrenaline, down to the smallest muscles at the base of each hair, your body reacts to fear.

Think about how you respond to fear spiritually. Things start to go wrong, do you question God? You get a terrible diagnosis. Do you worry God won't heal? Your marriage is torn apart because of infidelity. Do you feel anxious that God can't reconcile?

■ ■ ■

Fear can be debilitating or motivating, depending on how you respond to it.

■ ■ ■

Satan uses fear to stop you from trusting, from enjoying, from testifying, from loving, from having any joy in the freedom of God's truth.

Truth: Do Not be Afraid

Over 500 times, the word fear is used in the Bible. Here is my favorite truth God speaks over fear: "So do not fear, for I am with you; do not be dismayed, for I am your God. I will strengthen you and help you; I will uphold you with my righteous right hand" (Isaiah 41:10, NIV). "But now, this is what the Lord says— he who created you, Jacob, he who formed you, Israel: 'Do not fear, for I have redeemed you; I have summoned you by name; you are mine. When you pass through the waters, I will be with you; and when you pass through the rivers, they will not sweep over you. When you walk through the fire, you will not be burned; the flames will not set you ablaze'" (Isaiah 43:1-2, NIV).

■ ■ ■

Do not fear. Do not be afraid. Do not be anxious. Do not worry because God is God.

■ ■ ■

His strength is your strength. He is holding you. The same hands that formed you from dust uphold you. When you're passing through troubled waters, He is with you. You are His; He calls you by name. The same master Potter, the same breath that filled your lungs is your God. He will not let the waters sweep you up or the flames consume you. What then, can we possibly fear?

Doesn't the enemy say over and over again that we can't do something, that we aren't right or strong enough? Doesn't he whisper that we aren't loved or worthy or beautiful? Do you hear his slithering lies telling you that you aren't good enough?

Hear him for what he is, and that is a liar. He will steal the God-breathed breath out of your lungs and the God-promised joy out of your days. He will rob you of rest and happiness, but I need to tell you something, sweet friend. The truth of Jesus, the love He provides will shut down these lies in your life.

These lies we hear, the little voice in our head threatening our faith, it's human. It's our garden-chosen sin-nature to feel these things. The problem in our sinful hearts isn't that we think them, but the problem happens when we entertain them, when we actually start to believe them to be true. When we don't immediately replace them with what we know to be God's truth.

This struggle is daily for me. Lies like, "you aren't a good enough mom," "you could be happier if _____," "your struggles are your own," "you can't accomplish that," and I have this battle in my mind. Lies beat out by truth because I have learned to see the lies for what they are, the enemy trying to steal my life, my joy, and I know God's truth and promises will be victorious.

Reflection

o   What lies do you struggle with?

o   How can knowing God's truth help you cover the lies?

Prayer

Lord, your truth is so, so good. Your love for me is exactly what my heart needs. Your words bring peace to my soul when fear and lies creep in. Forgive me for trying to find fulfillment in anything but you. Forgive me for isolating myself, for thinking I'm alone, when you are right here with me. Forgive me for thinking I'm not loved when you have shown me in the biggest way that I am. Forgive me for fear that threatens faith, when I know that you have told me there is no reason to be afraid. Thank you for your truth and constant reminders of your love for me. God, help me to rely on you for these fears that I feel. I pray that your truth will sink into my heart and cover these lies.

Five

Battles

People often think that a life tethered to God would be immune to hardships. That pain-free life is the life He planned for us, but we chose wisdom and sin, and the perfect world He planned for us, was made imperfect. In this world, there is disease, there is divorce, there is addiction, there is infidelity, and there are battles.

I want to make clear that this life, full of struggles and heartbreak, is NOT the life He envisioned for His dust-made, God-breathed creation. The world He made for us was perfection, paradise. We were whole in uninterrupted communion with God, and it was beautiful.

■ ■ ■

The world He made for us was void of heartbreak and cancer and death.

■ ■ ■

But Satan's lies were too tempting, and with the bite of fruit, came battles on this earth.

The Bible is full of physical battles, one nation fighting another, but there are also spiritual battles for the soul, the enemy seeking death to the joy and freedom that Jesus won with his life.

There's a battle I remember learning about in Sunday School. We even sang the words in a musical performed for our small congregation. All these years later, I can still remember my duet of the song about this battle, though I had no idea then, what these words said about God. I'm sure off key, I sang the words, "Joshua fought the battle of Jericho, and the walls came tumbling down." The Battle of Jericho says so much about who God is, and shows His ability to fight for His people and bring the walls in your life tumbling down.

God gave Joshua his battle orders: "March around the city once with all the armed men. Do this for six days. Have seven priests carry trumpets of rams' horns in front of the ark. On the seventh day, march around the city seven times, with the priests blowing the trumpets" (Joshua 6:3-4, NIV).

Joshua did exactly what God commanded him to do. He didn't question the God who had delivered the Israelites, who made up his army, from captivity in Egypt. He had seen God rescue and provide and protect, so he didn't flinch when his battle orders were to march around the city and blow horns.

The ark that he was instructed to carry was the Ark of The Covenant, an ornate chest holding the tablets engraved with the Ten Commandments, a pot of manna, and the rod of Aaron. The Ark was a religious symbol, a place for people to meet with God. It symbolized His presence. The Ten Commandments that God gave Moses after leading the Israelites out of slavery. The pot of manna was a reminder of God's raining down of bread as provision for His people in the desert. The rod of Aaron that turned into a snake and turned water to blood and summoned plagues.

Joshua was not afraid because they were carrying the Ark, and in it was reminders of God's deliverance from slavery and fulfilled faithfulness to His people. God's presence was with them, as it had been.

I'm terrible with numbers, hence the English major, but I did some calculations and research about the wall surrounding Jericho. The wall built around the city of Jericho was circling around 9.88 acres of land. The wall was 11.8 feet high and 5.9 feet wide.

My brain shuts off when I see a lot of numbers and measurements, so I'll try to put the magnitude of that wall into words. The height of this wall was about two times as tall as a refrigerator. The width was almost as long as a full sized bed. For me, these help put the wall size into perspective. It was tall and wide and made of stone. It was made to keep people out. It was made to protect the people inside, but it wasn't too tall or too strong for an army with God's presence and favor.

"On the seventh day, they got up at daybreak and marched around the city seven times in the same manner, except that on that day they circled the city seven times. The seventh time around, when the priests sounded the trumpet blast, Joshua commanded the army, 'Shout! For the Lord has given you the city! The city and all that is in it are to be devoted to the Lord. Only Rahab the prostitute and all who are with her in her house shall be spared, because she hid the spies we sent. But keep away from the devoted things, so that you will not bring about your own destruction by taking any of them. Otherwise you will make the camp of Israel liable to destruction and bring trouble on it. All the silver and gold and the articles of bronze and iron are sacred to the Lord and must go into his treasury'" (Joshua 6:15-19, NIV).

Joshua did exactly what God told him to do for seven days. He commanded his army to shout because the city was theirs because he knew their God would fulfill His promise. "The Lord will fight for you; you need only to be still" (Exodus 14:14, NIV). The same God who broke the chains of Egypt was fighting for them, so Joshua was still and listened and waited.

I don't want to go into too much detail about Rahab because we will talk about who God chooses to use to build His Kingdom in a later chapter, but we can't go on without discussing the fact that God used a prostitute to hide the spies that helped correspond plans that led to victory. Rahab, a prostitute played a role in this great unfolding of God's power.

"When the trumpets sounded, the army shouted, and at the sound of the trumpet, when the men gave a loud shout, the wall collapsed; so everyone charged straight in, and they took the city. They devoted the city to the Lord and destroyed with the sword every living thing in it—men and women, young and old, cattle, sheep and donkeys. Joshua said to the two men who had spied out the land, 'Go into the prostitute's house and bring her out and all who belong to her, in accordance with your oath to her'" (Joshua 6:20-22, NIV).

The army of men didn't throw rocks at the wall or chisel away with tools. They shouted a cry of praise to their God, and the wall collapsed. Then they followed through with their promise to God to devote the city to Him and kept Rahab and her family safe for their faithfulness.

"So the Lord was with Joshua, and his fame spread throughout the land" (Joshua 6:27, NIV). So the Lord was with Joshua, and He is with you. Whatever battle you are facing, whatever walls you need to crumble, whatever force or army you feel is against you, trust that the God of Joshua is yours too. The God today is still the same God as then.

■ ■ ■

The same miraculous God who freed captives and kept promises and brought walls tumbling down; He remains.

■ ■ ■

And He didn't plan for you to fight battles when He created earth and a perfect Garden, but the choice was made. And He didn't plan for you to struggle trying to fight on your own. He didn't plan for your life to be full of battles, but the war for your soul is real; between a loving God with good plans and promised joy-filled eternity and an enemy who seeks destruction and eternal death.

In the many hardships and battles I have faced in my life, some chosen in sin and some a product of a sin-filled earth, I have learned that no wall is too high or too wide or too strong for God. I have learned to feel His presence and courageously shout praise. I have learned that no matter your past, He can and will use you to further His Kingdom. I have learned to blow trumpets and march in fellowship, to rely on the God who continually honors promises.

These battles won't always be huge walls or high mountains or dry desserts, but they can be mundane, everyday struggles. Joy in the diaper changes. Strength in the toddler tantrums. Praise in the flat tire. Trust in the unpaid bill. Patience in the potty-training. Grace in the rocky relationship. Selflessness in the washing of dishes.

■ ■ ■

Instead of being frustrated and angry and bitter with hardships, we need to learn from them.

■ ■ ■

From trouble, we can learn about ourselves and about God. From difficult circumstances, we see our incapability, our need for saving. From hard times, we see God is capable, always working, and always fighting for what is best for us.

"Have I not commanded you? Be strong and courageous. Do not be afraid; do not be discouraged, for the Lord your God will be with you wherever you go" (Joshua 1:9, NIV). Our flesh doubts and fear sets in, and we get discouraged because we feel we have lost, but God is with us. The Old Testament Ark is gone, and instead, His Spirit is in us. Cry out to the God who fulfills promises of saving and parts seas and rains bread and crumbles walls for His people.

If you start to doubt that He is with you in your battles, if you don't feel His presence in your circumstances, if your debt or marriage or friendships or job or financial struggles seem too big, repeat to yourself over and over the lyrics from my childhood song, "Joshua fought the battle of Jericho, and the walls came tumbling down." Shout praise and blow trumpets because his God is your God, and He is with you too.

Reflection

o   What battles are you facing?

o   How can you trust God more to crumble the walls in your life?

o   What can you learn about Him during battles?

Prayer

God, I know the life you planned for me was perfect; peaceful, whole, uninterrupted relationship with you. Forgive me for choosing sin over that. Thank you for being with me in the battles. Thank you for your power and strength to overcome any situation I am going through. I pray that you will comfort me, guide me, and crumble the walls that I am facing.

Six

Trust

We live in a valley, land surrounded by mountains, and when the wind blows, it really blows. On a fall night, the wind was literally howling, and my husband and I were watching a scary movie after we put the kids down for the night. I'm no good at watching scary movies; I mostly watch through my hand covered eyes, and jump and sweat and squeal during super scary parts, so when we heard a loud crash outside, needless to say, I was scared.

We looked out at the back porch of the house, where the noise came from, and saw the outdoor glass table hanging over the side of the porch, umbrella turned inside out and glass everywhere. I have never seen so many pieces of glass. The table was completely shattered into hundreds of thousands of pieces. On the porch our kids play. On the ground they run. On the steps they scoot down, and the thought of cleaning up every little piece was completely overwhelming. We decided to wait until the light of day to start the process of cleaning.

I spent hours, days, sweeping, vacuuming, picking up pieces by hand, and to this day, there are still shards of glass that I haven't found. The sharp, tiny pieces cut my fingers, and the broken mess just seemed to be too much, too shattered. As I picked up each individual piece of a once whole table, I realized how similar this situation was to another we have had in our lives.

Has someone ever broken your trust? So much like the shattered table, trust broken leaves you with an uncountable amount of pieces, sharp shards, once whole and smooth. Infidelity, lies of a friend, turning backs of family, a colleague now foe, these situations leave our trust shattered, but never beyond repair.

No matter our circumstances in life or relationships, we know that there is someone we can always trust. "Trust in the Lord with all your heart and lean not on your own understanding; in all your ways submit to him, and he will make your paths straight" (Proverbs 3:5-6, NIV).

■ ■ ■

Because the Lord is constant, never changing, always loving, you can trust Him without fear of hurt.

■ ■ ■

He is the only one who can be trusted completely because people are flawed, but He is perfect.

"When I am afraid, I put my trust in you. In God, whose word I praise— in God I trust and am not afraid. What can mere mortals do to me?" (Psalms 56:3-4, NIV). I just want to establish that your trust in God will not be shattered like the table. He will be your constant when the winds of this world are howling. You can trust Him with your life, your relationships, your needs. There is so much heartbreak in brokenness, broken trust. But with God, healing is possible, no matter the circumstance.

The dictionary definition of trust is the firm belief in the reliability, truth, ability, or strength of someone or something.

Although God will always be reliable, truthful, able, and strong, you can't hold people to those same standards. We fall short; over and over. So what happens when trust is shattered?

I know it is possible. For us, the rebuilt relationship was worth the work and time and healing, but there may be seasons where you feel the brokenness exceeds the time needed to rebuild, the effort not worth the risk. I can tell you that I was broken, my trust was broken, my husband's trust broken, into more pieces than our shattered glass table. I can't tell you who to trust or how to choose, but I am going to give you some very practical steps in rebuilding trust.

There is always a risk, a chance you take in trusting again because we all choose sin and ourselves by nature, but if we are trusting God and living a life redeemed, reflecting His love and Spirit, giving our brokenness to Him, then nothing is too shattered. You can't do it without Him, rebuilding trust takes selflessness and faith that can only come from His Spirit in you.

Steps to Rebuild Trust

1. Choose to Trust Again

I know this sounds crazy. But trusting someone is a choice, and without choosing to trust and choosing to put the time in to rebuild, you won't get anywhere. Stay in the present, thinking about the past or being angry about what may happen in the future will only keep your pieces in pieces.

Anytime I am having trouble trusting again, I try to train my brain. When a thought of distrust arises, I replace it with a thought of how my husband has provided or loved us recently. Our trust has been rebuilt, but Satan is not happy that he didn't win the battle for our marriage, and we're humans with insecurities and fear. Work together to be open and communicate about your struggles.

The only certainty in trusting people is that there is no certainty, no guarantee for a relationship without hurt. So, the first step to building trust is acknowledging that fact, and choosing to trust again, regardless.

2. Confess Your own Faults/Decide to Forgive

No one is perfect, and that's why we all need saving. We all fall short, and finger pointing will get you nowhere, actually it will just dig you deeper. Whatever your situation, think of ways or events or words you could have chosen differently, times you needed forgiveness.

It is a joy-filled feeling to be forgiven. We would all be condemned, daily, if not for grace undeserved, selfless blood shed. Our next chapter is on forgiveness so we will go into more detail then, but think, for now, about your debt paid, your redemption, your purpose made new.

Can we expect forgiveness without giving it in return? Forgiveness doesn't mean we accept their behavior or condone their choices, but instead, forgiving allows our heart to be at peace. It allows healing and the ability to trust again.

3. Be Honest

The only way to start rebuilding trust after lies, is to tell the truth. Over and over. speak the truth, and expect it in return. Focus on being consistent and look for that same consistency.

In every aspect of your life, your day, your thoughts, seek to tell the truth. You may hurt feelings, but truth telling will keep you on the path to rebuilding trust, and you should expect the same from the other person.

Luke 16:10 says, "If you are faithful in little things, you will be faithful in large ones" (NIV). Be honest in every little thing and expect that from the people in your life.

■ ■ ■

Building relationships on these little truths will pour foundation for a truthful and faithful future.

■ ■ ■

4. Pray, Pray, Pray

You cannot do this on your own. Bring your worries, your insecurities, your fears, your anger to God. Let His peace wash over you and pick you up piece by piece. Leave your inability at His feet and trust that He is working.

Pray for yourself, for healing and God's will in your circumstances. Pray for the other person and their hardships and heartbreak. Pray for God's power and restoration over your situation.

Pray as you drive or shower or cook dinner. Pray when you are anxious or fearful. Prayer in building trust will give you peace when flesh wants revenge.

5. Get in Shape

Rebuilding trust is a marathon, not a sprint. Condition yourself; get in shape because trust is rebuilt over time. You can't sprint through these steps and expect wholeness again. Train yourself like a marathon runner. Day after day, choose to trust again daily, confess your own sins, forgive because we are forgiven, be honest and consistent, and pray for God's peace in your situation.

Just like our table, trust rebuilt may never be the same, but it can be restored; it can be made new. Once broken, even when pieces are put back together, the product will be changed, more delicate, made fragile by howling winds. If you try on your own, you'll only be cut by the jagged edges.

■ ■ ■

Trust Jesus to pick up every single shard of brokenness and recreate something better, something whole, something rebuilt with Him as the foundation, the glue.

■ ■ ■

It's not easy, but loving relationships and trust and forgiveness and mercy undeserved are evidence of Jesus' power, a reflection of Christ in us. Testimony learned and lived and shared, the way that I am sharing with you.

There were so many times I felt my trust was too broken to continue. How could I ever trust again? My husband went through stages of anger and forgiveness and fear and distrust and healing. How could he ever trust again? There's fear of failure, shame in being fooled, anxiety about being hurt again, but even if the person fails, lies again, breaks trust again, you showed the light of Jesus. Your relationship with Him was restored, made deeper, trust learned in any circumstance, brokenness made whole again.

Choose to trust again. Jesus doesn't break promises. He is reliable and trustworthy and unfathomably mighty. Trust that He is protecting you. Know that with Him as the glue, your broken shards of trust can be, will be, made new.

Reflection

o   Has anyone ever broken your trust?

o   How do you struggle to trust again?

Prayer

Jesus, you are trustworthy. You are never changing; you always speak the truth because you are the Truth. It hurts when trust is broken. Forgive me for the ways I have broken trust. Forgive me for the sins in my own life. Thank you for being a constant when the world is full of change and broken trust. Please help me to choose to trust again. Help me to confess my own sin, when all I want to do is point fingers. Help me to be honest and prayerful in every situation. Please, Lord, give me strength and endurance to stick with the tough process of rebuilding trust.

Seven

Forgiveness

Since we have already talked about God's forgiveness of our sins and the redemption found at the cross, in this chapter, we're going to focus on our forgiving of others. Like trust, forgiveness requires work because our hearts break and people cause hurt and sin devastates.

We aren't God. We have trouble forgiving and throwing trespasses against us into the depths of the sea. Our sin nature wants to hold on to that wrongdoing, wallow in the hurt feelings, begrudgingly. But this is not what Jesus says to do when someone sins against us.

With three kids, we have conversations of forgiveness often. "She hit me!" "He tore my picture!" Or the kids act like they have no sense in the middle of Target and then come to me for forgiveness. We go through the motions of apologizing, the importance of saying, "I'm sorry," and then the opportunity for the other person to share the gift of forgiveness.

One day, our five and three year olds decided to make a particularly huge mess of the kitchen. Instead of waking me in the morning, they decided to do some cooking and mixing and experimenting with all of the condiments they could find in the fridge, along with the entire containers of garlic and onion powder from the pantry. And when I woke, the stench was unreal. A mix of ketchup and ranch and garlic greeted me from the kitchen. I can't lie to you; I lost my cool. It was just too much. The mess, the smell, the waste of food, and I banished the kids to the living room, so I could start cleaning this mess.

Our daughter lingered in the doorway, curls untamed and dimples deep, and with her precious voice, she put into practice what we have worked on over and over. She said, "I'm sorry, mom. Do you forgive me?" With utterly frustrated but incredibly proud tears in my eyes, I told her that I forgave her. And do you know how she responded? She said, "I forgive you too." And then went to sit on the couch with her brother where I told them both to sit until forever.

For a moment, I was angry, thinking she didn't understand forgiveness. After all the conversations we had discussing apologies and forgiveness, how could she still not understand? After all the words I spent explaining. After all the time I poured into teaching them this important faith and life concept, how could she still not get it? But as I scrubbed the ranch concoction covered floor, I realized. I realized that she understood forgiveness. In fact, she understood it more than me in that moment. Because she knew that

■ ■ ■

forgiveness is something that we need and accept and give, and we are called to do it freely, without question, with or without an apology for behavior.

■ ■ ■

Because my outburst definitely deserved an apology, in the same way as her science experiment. So, I went humbly to the living room, and I thanked her for her sincere apology and free forgiveness, and we started our day new.

The book of Matthew is full of conversations between Jesus and His disciples, about faith, morality, forgiveness, and sins. When reading this excerpt, remember that they were living during times of very strict Jewish law. The paid debt for sins was only attainable through certain rituals and courses of action, the law stating to forgive only three times. So, when Peter asked Jesus, "'Lord, how many times shall I forgive my brother or sister who sins against me? Up to seven times?,'" he thought that he was granting over twice the mercy that the law required (Matthew 18:21, NIV).

But, "Jesus answered, 'I tell you, not seven times, but seventy-seven times" (Matthew 18:22, NIV). His response indicates that there is no amount to be exceeded when it comes to forgiving. Wouldn't you lose count after 490 times?

■ ■ ■

*There is no ruled number
because there is no counting, no
keeping score of wrongs done.*

■ ■ ■

Then, Jesus tells this eye opening parable about a master and servant and debt paid.

"'Therefore, the kingdom of heaven is like a king who wanted to settle accounts with his servants. As he began the settlement, a man who owed him ten thousand bags of gold was brought to him.

Since he was not able to pay, the master ordered that he and his wife and his children and all that he had be sold to repay the debt.

'At this the servant fell on his knees before him. 'Be patient with me,' he begged, 'and I will pay back everything.' The servant's master took pity on him, canceled the debt and let him go" (Matthew 18:23-27, NIV).

So, this servant owed the king ten thousand bags of gold, a debt the servant was sure to never make even in a lifetime of work. It was an unpayable debt. But, when the king orders for the servant and his wife and children to be sold to pay the amount, the servant begged for mercy.

Our debt is unpayable. The qualification for eternity in heaven is perfection, and we can never give that, no amount of good works or volunteering, no life spent serving will equal that sum because we are sinners in birth. You can't go back in time and be perfect from the beginning.

■ ■ ■

Even if you seek to sin less, you definitely can't be sinless.

■ ■ ■

In the same way the master took pity and canceled the debt of the servant, God sent Jesus to cancel ours. He didn't set up a payment plan, credit given with interest, or sell us for a fraction of the payment, He wiped the slate completely clean because that was the only way we could receive the Promised Land.

"'But when that servant went out, he found one of his fellow servants who owed him a hundred silver coins. He grabbed him and began to choke him.

'Pay back what you owe me!' he demanded. 'His fellow servant fell to his knees and begged him, 'Be patient with me, and I will pay it back.' 'But he refused.

Instead, he went off and had the man thrown into prison until he could pay the debt. When the other servants saw what had happened, they were outraged and went and told their master everything that had happened.

'Then the master called the servant in, 'You wicked servant,' he said, 'I canceled all that debt of yours because you begged me to. Shouldn't you have had mercy on your fellow servant just as I had on you?' In anger his master handed him over to the jailers to be tortured, until he should pay back all he owed.

'This is how my heavenly Father will treat each of you unless you forgive your brother or sister from your heart'" (Matthew 18:28-35, NIV).

So, this servant who just experienced unfathomable mercy, this servant who was about to be sold alongside his family, but then was granted the forgiveness of his debt, leaves the king's presence and refused that same mercy to a fellow servant, and that servant only owed him a hundred silver coins. In anger, he choked the other servant, and when the debted servant fell on his knees to beg for patience and time, his pleas were met with prison and chains.

Word spread quickly, and the master brought the forgiven, but unforgiving servant back, calling him wicked. He questioned him, how can you accept forgiveness and then deny that same mercy to another? Then, the once free servant was sentenced to prison and torture until the debt was paid.

If our sin is our debt, and God's law requires perfection, then our debt is too great for us to ever pay, even in a lifetime of trying to do good, you would always come up short. God knew this. Our begging and pleas are repeatedly met with mercy and forgiveness, so why, then, do we struggle so much with the forgiving of others?

■ ■ ■

If we expect forgiveness of our sins, then we too need to be compassionate and mercy-filled when it is our turn to do the forgiving.

■ ■ ■

Only days after the night my sin was brought to light, my husband agreed to meet with me at a local park. As I parked my car, I saw him. I saw him for the first time since that night. For the first time since my betrayal. For the first time since his rage and hurtful words.

He was sitting at a picnic table; he didn't look at me as I walked over, my own head down, hung in shame. I fell to my knees at his feet, and I managed to choke out a tearful, "I'm so sorry." With undeserved kindness, he asked me to get up, and he invited me to sit at the table with him. He wasn't smiling, but I could tell there was something different about him. He didn't look unhappy or full of hate; he just looked at peace.

As he spoke, I barely recognized him. He said that in all of this pain and suffering, through panic attacks and rage, God had found him and given him peace and the ability to love and forgive. He prayed for our talk, for our kids, and for me. He apologized for not being the leader, the husband, the dad that God called him to be. Not condoning my sins, but admitting his own.

I cried and apologized and apologized, never feeling like I could express how deeply sorry I was for shutting God out, giving up, and making this selfish mistake. No amount of "sorry" could ever be enough for the pain I knew I caused him.

We talked for hours, neither of us wanting to leave, almost a decade spent together made it even more difficult when the person you normally confide in was the one that causes the hurt. As the sun started to move behind the trees, we scheduled my first visit with the kids for the next day, and we hugged, clinging to each other and the promises of a good God.

This wasn't the end of the battle for our marriage, the devil persistently seeking to destroy and God faithfully seeking to reconcile. It was really only the beginning of a years long fight. When light was shed to my husbands' own struggles with sin and affairs, I remembered the grace that was given to me. I was alone, raising our kids, wondering where he was, tears spilled mourning the joy and reconciliation that was in reach. Every human part of me wanted to yell and scream and wallow in the pain of his lies, but instead, I met him with the same mercy undeserved. The same forgiveness and grace granted, unpayable debt wiped clean. It wasn't easy; daily, I chose to trust again and forgive again because I knew what God expected of me, what God continually grants me. I knew that feeling of forgiven debt, and I wanted so desperately to give it in return.

After my infidelity, I wanted so much to be forgiven by my husband and family and friends. I begged and pleaded, knowing my debt was more than I could ever imagine repaying. I'm so incredibly blessed that loved ones in my life know what it feels like to be forgiven and gave that same mercy in return. But how easy it would have been for their flesh to cast me out, grow angry at my begging, refuse to forgive my sins.

I don't know who you are struggling to forgive. I don't know the hurt that they caused you, the tears you have shed, the nights spent tossing instead of resting, the attacks of panic and anxiety that their actions afflicted you with, but I do know the peace that is possible in praying and surrendering and choosing to forgive in Jesus' name.

Whether it's a child choosing to make a mess or live in a way that you did not teach them, or parents who spoke harshly, or the siblings who are not perfect, or the friends who made plans without you, or the husband who doesn't treat you the way he's called to, or the boss who rarely gives praise, or the stranger who cut out in front of you and raised a certain finger.

If we want to continue being forgiven, then we have to forgive. Forgive, as you are forgiven, and instead of meeting the pleas of a child or parent or friend or spouse or stranger with anger and harshness, show them the forgiving love of Jesus.

Forgiveness is hard. Flesh wants to wallow. Fear wants to hold grudge. Lay your struggles with forgiving at the feet of Jesus. If you feel bitter at forgiving someone who is underserving, forgive. If the pain they caused you feels like it's too much to bear, forgive. If your pride is saying you don't deserve this, forgive. Even if you know you're right, forgive.

Listen to the whispers of Jesus, reminding you of your own undeserved redemption, your own unpayable debt paid. Show Jesus' love to the people who feel unlovable; reach the unreachable with the joy given when the words, "I forgive you," are uttered.

There is power in forgiveness, bitterness replaced, prisoners set free. Grace-filled eyes are able to see that we are the prisoner whose chains are broken. Forgiving others sets our hearts free from a life that would be otherwise chained by hate and grudge and bitterness.

"Bear with each other and forgive one another if any of you has a grievance against someone. Forgive as the Lord forgave you" (Colossians 3:13, NIV). Forgive as you have been forgiven, freely and without grudge.

■ ■ ■

Toss your grievances into the depths, where Jesus sinks your sins daily.

■ ■ ■

Reflection

o   Who/why arc you struggling to forgive?

o   How can you greet that person with mercy?

Prayer

God, you forgive so freely, with no record of wrongs, sins cast into the depths of the sea. Forgive me for the sins that separate me from you. Forgive me for not forgiving, when you have forgiven me over and over. Thank you for chance after chance and your love for me regardless. Thank you for my debt wiped clean. Please help me to forgive the people who have hurt me. Apology or not, Jesus, help me to let go of the anger in my heart, so that I can be more like you.

Eight

Audience of One

I'm a people pleaser by nature. I think this stems from my parents' divorce and the need to make everyone happy amidst visitation agreements and child support and shared holidays. My need to please people is so engraved in my personality. We talked briefly in a previous chapter about the Enneagram personality test, and I explained a little bit about my personality as a Type 2. I hope by now you took that test because it really just gives so much insight. Anyway, here is how the Enneagram institute describes my personality: "Twos are empathetic, sincere, and warm-hearted. They are friendly, generous, and self-sacrificing, but can also be sentimental, flattering, and people-pleasing" (ennegraminstitute.com).

People-pleasing. People pleasing people tend to agree with everyone because they want to be liked; they apologize often, even when they didn't do anything wrong. They are overly sensitive to criticism; they have trouble saying "no" to others, and they are obsessed with what other people think about them. What I have learned over the last season of my life is that

■ ■ ■

trying to please other people is not living a life dedicated to pleasing Jesus. You can't seek to do both.

■ ■ ■

In putting weight solely in their applause. Love them, yes, but love them to please Him. Living to please people will leave you feeling like a failure because people are impossible to please.

My husband and I both had so many voices calling out to us in those first days and in the months and even years to come. Some advised divorce, some on doing the best for the kids, some on working on the marriage, and amidst all the voices, I begged for His to be the loudest, the clearest because people will always have opinions. But the only opinion, the only voice, the only advice I have decided to follow wholeheartedly is His. We talked to our pastor and counselors and family, and sometimes their suggestions aligned with what I could hear, feel God telling me to do. And sometimes the advice went against the gentle leading I knew to be His. Wise counsel from others can absolutely be directed from God, I'm not denying that, but if you tune your ears to His voice, you will be able to decipher between Biblical wisdom and flesh driven advice.

If I'm being honest, this was the hardest chapter for me to write because it is something that I struggle with every day. I researched and prayed and even as I wrote, situations came up where I found myself worrying about the pleasing of others instead of my audience of One. The two aspects of choosing an audience of One that I want to focus on in this chapter, the ones I feel speak to my heart most, are your actions and intentions and the applause or voices that you choose to listen to.

Actions and Intentions

■ ■ ■

Your life is made up of decisions that lead to actions and there are intentions behind those.

■ ■ ■

We need to purposefully, daily, prayerfully choose to make decisions within the will of God, and make sure that our intention in following is to please Him, not the people watching. Let your intention be to further His Kingdom, show His grace, His love.

I want to look at a passage in the Bible where Jesus comments on people who aim to please people instead of Him. These events, these actions depicted are just six days before the death and burial of Jesus. He had just raised Lazarus from the dead, and Martha hosted a dinner for him.

"Six days before the Passover, Jesus came to Bethany, where Lazarus lived, whom Jesus had raised from the dead. Here a dinner was given in Jesus' honor. Martha served, while Lazarus was among those reclining at the table with him. Then Mary took about a pint of pure nard, an expensive perfume; she poured it on Jesus' feet and wiped his feet with her hair. And the house was filled with the fragrance of the perfume.

But one of his disciples, Judas Iscariot, who was later to betray him, objected, 'Why wasn't this perfume sold and the money given to the poor? It was worth a year's wages.' He did not say this because he cared about the poor but because he was a thief; as keeper of the money bag, he used to help himself to what was put into it.

'Leave her alone,' Jesus replied. 'It was intended that she should save this perfume for the day of my burial. You will always have the poor among you, but you will not always have me'" (John 12:1-8, NIV).

There are so many things to break down in this chapter of John, and I don't want to miss a thing. I can't imagine the weight that Jesus was feeling only six days before his death, his time on earth ending. He knew his time was near, yet he chose to sit and eat. Jesus spent his life performing miracles and had just raised Lazarus from the dead, now they sat together at the same table, and I get chills. To sit and eat with the man capable of breathing life into death. What a privilege to know Him.

Mary washing Jesus' feet would not have been uncommon, as it was common for a guest's feet to be washed with water and their head anointed with a drop of oil or perfume when they entered the home. However, Mary used a pound of very expensive oil, which was worth more than a year's wages for work. Mary's gift to Jesus was humble, the humility of washing another person's feet. Her action was extreme in the costly oil, and her decision reflects a life lived to please Jesus. And the house was filled with the lingering aroma. With this humble action, Mary only hoped to please Jesus, but it fills the entire home with a sweet smell, illustrating the spreading of His goodness to others, His kingdom, even when the intention was to serve Him.

Judas objected because the oil was too expensive, making an excuse that the money should have been given to the poor, but this genuine and unselfish act of Mary, wasn't done to please people. She didn't care if anyone approved or even saw this gesture of praise. She chose to please Jesus. She chose to ignore what anyone else might have to say. She chose to put aside the negativity surrounding her King and sit at His feet, to honor him and surrender her life to His purpose. Oh, how I want to live a life reflecting Mary's.

■ ■ ■

Hush the audience of others and hear the applause of Jesus.

■ ■ ■

Jesus defends Mary, telling Judas to leave her alone, that Mary was honoring Him in what he knew were his last days.

"Meanwhile a large crowd of Jews found out that Jesus was there and came, not only because of him but also to see Lazarus, whom he had raised from the dead. So the chief priests made plans to kill Lazarus as well, for on account of him many of the Jews were going over to Jesus and believing in him" (John 12:9-11, NIV). The chief priests didn't believe in resurrection, so Lazarus alive after death threatened their belief system and was an embarrassment. These people who witnessed the miracles of Christ now plotting his death because of the fear of their tarnished image.

"Yet at the same time many even among the leaders believed in him. But because of the Pharisees they would not openly acknowledge their faith for fear they would be put out of the synagogue; for they loved human praise more than praise from God" (John 12:42-43, NIV). Some of the leaders could no longer deny His majesty, His Father, His power over the grave, but they wouldn't admit it openly because they were afraid. They were afraid of the opinion of others. They wanted the praise and acceptance of a human crowd more than the eternal praises from God.

My obsession to please people, that deep longing to make everyone else happy, to say "yes," and want for them to approve of me, harmed my marriage. I cared more about what other people wanted and said, and I denied the pleas of my husband. He wanted out of a work situation, but I wanted to make everyone else happy. I made decisions to not sympathize with my husband, and my actions sought to please people, and it led to so many issues in our already shaky marriage. Putting the opinions of other people before my kids and my husband and putting aside the selflessness that would have been pleasing to God. I didn't pray for God's will or wisdom in how to navigate the situation in a way that would be pleasing to Him; I grasped at straws and quick fixes and attempted to play mediator and tried to patch holes in relationships and denied enormous issues.

This life we are living needs to be one lived with the intention of pleasing Jesus by our love for others and following Him. Loving them does not mean that you are pleasing them always, but showing them unconditional love and constant forgiveness and Christ-given grace. Living for an audience of One means that He is the one we aim to please with our breath of a life on this earth. I desperately want to be a Mary instead of a Judas.

■ ■ ■

I want to spend my days honoring Him, kneeling at His feet, pouring out my last drops or entire bottle, smelling the sweet, sweet aroma, knowing my decisions and actions and intentions are to please Him.

■ ■ ■

Not questioning selfishly and hiding faith out of fear of people. "I'm not trying to win the approval of people, but of God. If pleasing people were my goal, I would not be Christ's servant" (Galatians 1-10, NLT). The problem with living a life intended on pleasing other people is that they, then, are the thing you are serving.

If you're living a life serving other people, you will feel rejected, your soul will be drained, and your work will certainly never be finished.

■ ■ ■

Putting people in a position of power in your life, choosing, thinking, and pursuing the adoration and praise from that idol, will not leave your soul-full or joy-filled.

■ ■ ■

Instead, live your life for an audience of One. One God who doesn't love you because you are good, or because you always follow directions, or because you wear certain clothes, or because you always say "yes," but simply because you're you.

His unconditional acceptance frees us from people pleasing. His continuously choosing us allows freedom from a life spent floundering and failing in the efforts to make people happy. God didn't create people to fulfill each other, that's only His ability. He created us to love and enjoy and celebrate and grieve, for fellowship in this life.

In my marriage, and in my roles as a mother, friend, sister, daughter, if I washed dishes or brought dinner or sent flowers or planned a surprise with the sole intention to please the people in my life, then I'm loving them for the wrong reasons. The selfless acts in our life, the actions of love need to be aimed at pleasing the One who gives us the strength to do them. Days are long and patience is short, and if we're expecting "thank you's" or applause from people, those expectations will not always be met.

■ ■ ■

If you are living to please Him, His approval of us frees us from the opinions of others.

■ ■ ■

"Whatever you do, work at it with all your heart, as working for the Lord, not for human masters, since you know that you will receive an inheritance from the Lord as a reward. It is the Lord Christ you are serving"(Colossians 3:23-24, NIV). Days and weeks seem long, but this life is short, and the opinions of others are fleeting, but a life spent pleasing God will give you the inheritance of Heaven. Choose to serve and please Christ and spread the aroma of His love.

Applause

If we focus on what people say about us, we forget what God says, and that's the identity we need to know and believe to be true. His opinion of us is the one worth abiding by. There was a time in my life where everyone had something to say about who I was. Whispers, comments, judging eyes, and in those moments, I chose to listen to my audience of One. I chose to hear Him saying I was redeemed, dust made new, sinner forgiven, prisoner set free. My prayer was for God's voice to be louder than any other, hearing Him was the most important thing because the opinions of others only sought to tear me down. Check your heart and make sure that His opinion of you is the one that matters most. Hear His voice louder than the shame and guilt and judgement of others.

"My sheep listen to my voice; I know them, and they follow me" (John 10:27, NIV). Here we are represented by sheep again, but it's so, so true. We wander off, and how thankful I am that He is my Shepherd, and I can hear his loving voice when I'm surrounded by darkness, and I can follow Him in faith to safety.

"You're a doormat," "You're a bad mom," "You deserve the worst," "You're wrong," "You're a failure," "You're too broken," "You will never accomplish _____," "You aren't pretty," "You're too Religious," "You should do _____," "You aren't doing _____ right."

Have you heard these voices? Have you let these people, these voices become your audience? The applause you listen for? As women, it's so hard to compare and see perfectly fit and clothed and make-upped celebrities, or even other moms at Target with the side-eye when your child is throwing a tantrum mid-shopping trip. Sometimes the voice is my own. Comparing: her house is perfectly clean, and she did a craft with her kids today, and I struggled with enough patience to just get through the day. Whispers of my mistakes and the shame and guilt and the fear of what people might say, these thoughts, this audience threatens to "boo" me right off the stage.

But, listen to what He says about you, about me. Imagine these are the words encouraging you to continue. Write them down. Put them in places where your eyes will see and your ears will hear the applause of Jesus, cheered before you were born, shouted even in sin, a standing ovation from the King.

You are a "child of God." You are a "branch of the true vine." You are justified and redeemed. You are free from sin and death. You are accepted. You are wise and righteous and sanctified. You are fearfully and wonderfully made. (John 1:12, John 15:5, Romans 8:1-2, 1 Corinthians 1:30, Psalm 139:14, NIV).

People say you're forsaken, forgotten, unworthy, weak, unable. Jesus says because of His love and sacrifice for you, you are forgiven, treasured, worthy, purposed, able. Believe what He says about you.

In the arena of this life, it doesn't matter if the seats are full. It doesn't matter if the crowd is on their feet clapping. It doesn't matter if their cheering is ringing in your ears. Hear me sweet friend,

■ ■ ■

His presence in your audience, His one seat filled is all that you need.

■ ■ ■

Living your life with actions and intentions to please Him, will fill the arena with all of the praise and adoration that you will ever need. Tune your ears to hear His praise, His voice, His applause in your life spent following His will for you.

I'll tell you that choosing to live for an audience of One can do the opposite of please people because they want to be heard and listened to, and there is no harm in allowing that, but you have to then check that with what you hear God advising. You might not always audibly hear him, but if you're spending time in His Word, seeking counsel from people you know follow His voice, and praying fervently that He shows you His will, I believe that you will feel peace in your decisions, even if the people around you aren't always pleased.

The opinions and approval of others is something that I still struggle with, but daily brought to the feet of Jesus, a habit forms, deep rooted faith and knowledge of His voice, and his ability in your inabilities, and His perfection in your flaws grant you peace. Ask for His strength and ability to be purposeful in your actions, to be a Mary and pour the oil, knowing unashamedly so that you are honoring Jesus.

"So whether we are at home or away, we make it our aim to please him" (2 Corinthians 5:9, ESV). The Judas' of this life will comment, snicker even, but this is my prayer. For my life and yours, living a life spent pouring the oil.

Reflection

o   Are you a Mary or a Judas?

o   Do you find yourself worrying about what others say about your actions?

o   What audience do you seek to hear praise from?

Prayer

God, you are the reason for life. You give me breath and purpose and calling. Forgive me for actions and intentions that are aimed at pleasing others. Thank you for your applause. Thank you for the ways that your approval fills my heart. I pray that you will help me love others, but in doing so, please you. Help me to train my ears for your applause, and know that it is all I need.

Nine

Fellowship

Growing up, I never asked what the word fellowship meant. It's one of those Church words that I heard and never really thought about. I knew it was something we did at church and there was even a whole building dedicated to it. In that fellowship hall, we ate and played and held most church events. It was a fun place full of joy and food and talking.

As I've grown older, I have come to know the true meaning, the true feeling, the true need for fellowship in this life. It's not just a building, and it's more than shared beliefs. It's more than just a potluck lunch on a Sunday afternoon. It's more than shaking hands and casual, "hello's." It's more than the comment that you'll be praying on someone's Facebook post. The goal of fellowship is to make us more like Christ, a glimpse of Heaven on earth.

There have been some seriously soul shattering seasons of my life that fellowship has helped piece back together. My faith grew in my hardest moments, but fellowship lifted me up when I could barely stand on my own. I will never forget the way that women who were just friends became sisters in Christ because they mirrored His grace and love, and their prayers gave me peace, their words, their wisdom, their continually pointing me to Christ. Fellowship has saved my life over and over again. It's the friend who stops the conversation and prays for the circumstance you're facing. It's the mom who serves your family when you can't. It's the woman trusting God's work in your life and reminding you of His goodness, even when you can't see. It's the friend who sees sin, but has arms open wide because of grace.

■ ■ ■

It's love that is unconditional in a world full of conditions.

■ ■ ■

I want to look at a letter that Paul sent to the church of Philippi. It breaks down exactly what fellowship, in Jesus' name, looks like. From his prison chains, his heart burst words of thankfulness to the people who didn't give up on him. His letter is to the people he poured his saved soul into, testified to, and brought to Jesus. The people who he had true biblical fellowship with. Paul's letter was addressed to quite possibly the first ever "church plant" and a church that many years later was used as a model for other churches. We're going to talk about five defining principles of fellowship that we can learn from Paul's letter and what this looks like in our own lives.

"(3) I thank my God every time I remember you. (4) In all my prayers for all of you, I always pray with joy (5) because of your partnership in the gospel from the first day until now, (6) being confident of this, that he who began a good work in you will carry it on to completion until the day of Christ Jesus. (7) It is right for me to feel this way about all of you, since I have you in my heart and, whether I am in chains or defending and confirming the gospel, all of you share in God's grace with me. (8) God can testify how I long for all of you with the affection of Christ Jesus. (9) And this is my prayer: that your love may abound more and more in knowledge and depth of insight, (10) so that you may be able to discern what is best and may be pure and blameless for the day of Christ, (11) filled with the fruit of righteousness that comes through Jesus Christ—to the glory and praise of God" (Philippians 1:3-11, NIV).

Can you hear his love and thankfulness for these people? In his prison cell, he is writing joyfully and heartfelt. I love that Paul says, "MY God." His relationship with God was that personal, and it's that personal relationship with the Savior that allows him to have fellowship with these people. Fellowship is so soul-filling because it's God given; it's capable of lifting you up, even when you're in chains, God's love shown through other people. It's a heavenly embrace on earth. It's why He gave Adam, Eve, and it's why God gave us each other. He made us, and He knew what our hearts desperately needed. He knew we would need fellowship in this life outside of the garden.

1. Fellowship is praying for one another (Verse 4)

Paul starts the letter by saying how he spends time praying for the people of Philippi. Don't we say to people all the time, "I'll be praying!" Or comment the praying hands emoji on Facebook, but are we actually taking those requests to the King? I hate to admit it, but sometimes I just say that, and then no words are uttered, and I want to get more intentional in praying for the people in my life. Because fellowship doesn't mean that you aren't also facing difficult circumstances; Paul is in literal physical chains. Fellowship by prayer for one another doesn't ignore the fact that you're busy, and you need to work and clean and make dinner. Fellowship by prayer for one another is defined by the fact that we're all struggling, and despite that, choosing to take the time to pray for someone else, Jesus' selfless love shown on earth.

If I were Paul, I would have prayed day and night for my own freedom, for my own hardships and needs. But Paul had faith that

God was working and would keep him safe, and that knowing freed him to pray for others. And he didn't just pray for them, he prayed with JOY. It doesn't say he prayed as he fell asleep or mumbled while he completed other tasks; he prayed with joy, purposefully, intentionally, fellowship through prayer with a body of people who weren't even physically near him because

■　■　■

fellowship unites us in Jesus, despite our physical circumstances.

■　■　■

Most of my friends are moms to young children, and days with little ones are full. Full to the brim with errands and cleaning and tantrums and cooking and diapering, and they probably barely had a minute to even pray for themselves. But when my friends said to me during my difficult circumstances that they were praying for me, I knew that they were sincere because I felt that overwhelming peace. Their lives were still busy, and we didn't see each other daily or even weekly, but one of my sweet friends would take the time to type out the prayer over text. Sometimes, instead of attending the church service on Sunday, we would find a quiet place and just sit and cry and pray together. There was a worship service at a women's conference that I remember so clearly. A friend who has loved me at all times kneeling at the altar in worship and fellowship with me praying and thanking God for our friendship, for what He has done and will do, and if you have ever had this, you know that overwhelming feeling of joy that comes with praying for and with your people. It's coming together, hearts redeemed, joyful prayers to the King.

My prayer for you, as my sister in Christ, is that you find people to fellowship with in this life. I can promise you that I stopped writing right here. I stopped to intentionally pray for you. I stopped to pray that you find your church and your people that God will use to encourage you and lift you up through prayer. I stopped to pray that you will find love in this life and learn more about Jesus. I stopped to pray that you will be able to hear and discern His voice and cling desperately to your Shephard. I stopped to pray joyfully for you, and I pray that you can feel that peace.

2. Fellowship is serving God together (Verse 5)

When Paul started the Philippian church, the members were active in serving the Lord, working together, sharing His goodness, serving each other in His name. Paul uses the words "partnership in the Gospel" to describe his relationship with the recipients of this letter. Their partnership in the gospel is defined by serving God together, and that fellowship means that they are partners in life. Partners in chains; partners in joy; partners in eternity.

I have been someone who just went to church; walk in, drop the kids off, grab coffee and a seat. Over the last year, I felt called to serve, to do more than simply attend. And I can tell you that the years spent simply attending were lacking the fellowship and soul-filling that serving has brought me.

Whether it's helping with the coffee bar, or the information table, or handing out bulletins, I know that it's fellowship. There's a warming of my heart that silences the bitter wind when I help with the greeting and opening of doors, even in the coldest months. I have met so many amazing men and women of God, and we get to serve Him together.

Sometimes you feel it's easier to just slip in and out, and your list of things to do is long, and your week was hard, but the gift of fellowship comes with serving. God saved you and me in love to serve Him.

■ ■ ■

Serving Him isn't always convenient or easy, but it brings us closer in fellowship when we join together in serving Him.

■ ■ ■

Taking your time to serve others makes your heart more like Jesus. Choosing to put others before ourselves shows Jesus' selfless love, and isn't our goal to be more like Him? To live a life reflecting redemption?

As I typed this, I got a message from a woman who has shown me love and grace over and over asking me to serve by greeting and opening doors on Sunday, and it just made me smile because isn't God amazing in that way? I'm writing about choosing to serve God together, and I get a message about the opportunity to do that. Over and over He gives me validation and clear guidance in ways that I can serve Him by serving others.

After my sin was brought to light, I really wanted to just fade into the background at church. I wanted to be there so desperately, but I didn't want to be seen. That part of my life was really focused on just being there and worshiping and thanking God for redeeming me. But now, I'm opening doors and smiling and greeting people and handing out bulletins without fear of judgment or whispers because I know who I am in Him, and I will give all of myself to His service. Because He saved me. Because He loves me. Because His plan for me is good, and my time spent serving Him with others is a piece of Heaven on earth; souls redeemed choosing to serve and praise Him together is a glimpse of our eternity in Heaven.

3. Fellowship is trusting in and reminding of God's work in each other (Verse 6)

I love this part of fellowship. It's the friend who you confide in. The mom who answers your call daily, quietly listening and pointing you continually to Jesus. The woman you trust with a situation, and you tell her what God is showing you, or maybe you don't even know what God is doing. You're in the middle of a storm and there are no clear skies in sight, but this sweet sweet friend reminds you that HE IS WORKING.

Over and over and over my best friends sat with me as I cried and updated them on the circumstances of my life. There were so many times they didn't have an answer. They were in tears too; their hands up in disbelief or unknowing, but each time, they would remind me. They would point me back to Jesus;

■ ■ ■

you might not understand the storm or see the clear skies, but the rainbow is coming.

■ ■ ■

Just like Paul said, God started the work, and He will complete it. And fellowship is having people to surround you, to over and over again remind you that He is not done; that His plan is good and the chains will be broken, and the storm will be calmed because He is good. People who speak Romans 8:28 over your life and into your soul when you need reminding, "And we know that in all things God works for the good of those who love him, who have been called according to his purpose" (Romans 8:28, NIV).

4. Fellowship is accepting God's grace together (Verse 7)

Days after my sin was brought to light, I got a text from an amazing woman in my life, inviting me to her home to talk. I was so scared. I was so nervous, and I just wanted to hide. I called my mom as I drove over to alleviate some of my anxiety, and I expressed that I just felt like I needed to talk to this sweet friend. She had been a mentor to me; over the years, her farm was a home I knew I could escape to and just find Jesus. My heart broke knowing I needed to confess my sin and shame around the same table where I spent many Tuesdays learning and growing spiritually with other women.

When I walked to her door, she was crouched in her entryway, Bible open; palms up. When she saw me, she ran to the door with a beaming smile. The joy on her face was that of the shepherd's neighbors rejoicing; she greeted me with the grateful embrace of a sheep brought safely home, and I will never forget the feeling of grace overwhelming me. This friend who could have turned me away, shamed me, hated me, opened her arms instead.

She offered me coffee, and we sat at her kitchen island. I started from the beginning; confessing how it came to this. I did the laundry, cooked, cleaned, raised the kids, paid the bills, cared for everyone, and when I stopped relying on God for the strength, I broke. I cried as I told her. There was no excuse for what I did, but this was how I got there- to that place of darkness and desperation. I wanted attention, someone to love me, something new and fun, something for me. Her face never turned to judgement; her eyes never turned to hate. This moment defined fellowship for me.

Her heart, full of Jesus, offering grace and unconditional love in my most vulnerable and exposed time. I felt God brought me to her at that exact moment to show me His love through this treasured friend. Fellowship is acknowledging that I have accepted God's grace, and then giving that to others, at their worst moment or their best, reflecting the heart of Jesus and rejoicing together in this undeserved gift.

"As iron sharpens iron, so a friend sharpens a friend" (Proverbs 27:17, NLT). This gift of fellowship and accepting God's grace together sharpens us, and just as iron is used to sharpen iron, it makes us more like Jesus, forgiving and loving and acknowledging our need for grace to be received and then given.

5. Fellowship is genuine heartfelt love for one another (Verse 8)

Paul calls upon God as a witness to his longing and loving affection for the people of the Philippian Church. He says that God can testify, the God who knows his heart completely, could testify to his love for them. He wasn't bitter that they were free. He wasn't angry that they weren't doing more. His heart was full of affection. The words Paul uses are the "affection of Christ Jesus." There are two different definitions of the word affection: a gentle feeling of fondness or liking, and the act or process of being affected; by a disease, mental state, or emotion. And this word just really illustrates how we are called to love each other in fellowship.

■ ■ ■

It's a guttural affliction of affection, the whole-hearted, unselfish love and sacrifice of Jesus.

■ ■ ■

It's a mental state, a heart changed, redeemed souls seeking to love like Jesus. It's scary to love people this much because this world is full of sin, but we are called to and defined by our love for others.

■ ■ ■

Our relationship with Him grants us the ability to unite in a world that seeks to divide.

■ ■ ■

This love isn't manipulative. It doesn't have self-serving motives. It is love despite personal inconvenience or sacrifice. It is genuine, heartfelt, cross inspired love for one another. This love builds people up.

The best way for me to relate to this type of love is through motherhood. My kids, they challenge me daily. They paint the walls with yogurt. They unroll all of the toilet paper. They throw toys in the toilet. They wipe boogers on my clean shirt. But they smile and my heart feels joy. They laugh, and I want to laugh with them. They cry, and I kiss their worries or boo-boos away. My own mom was hurt by my sinful actions, but she never stopped loving me. And I think this is the most earth-like example of Christs' unconditional love for each other.

In the same way we are called to Christ-like unconditional love in marriage and motherhood and family, we are also called to it in friendship and fellowship because the Bible tells us that "a friend loves at all times" (Proverbs 17:17, NIV). One of my sweet friends sent this verse to me in a text days after my sin was exposed. Her sending these words meant that her love for me was not conditional. Her love for me wasn't based on my perfection, but remained even in my imperfection. Her love for me is evident in good times and bad, and the only way we can love like this is through a relationship with the only One able to do this perfectly. Loving each other is not always easy. People sin and disappoint and feelings are hurt and some people might just get on your nerves. This principle of fellowship gives us the opportunity to show and feel Jesus' deep love and affection for the people in our lives.

Like Paul, I have this group of people to fellowship with in my life. This story is mine. This letter is mine. Writing from the chains of my sin, the dark cell, the walls containing me, and people still loving, still reaching out, still praying, still called, by the same God who saved me, into fellowship with me.

Please, please hear me. If you don't have this in your life, this God given gift of fellowship, you are missing out on a glimpse of Heaven on earth. You aren't receiving the gift given by the King, planned and designed because of His knowledge of our hearts' need to be in fellowship with others. If you don't know where to start, find a church. Pray for God to show you the way to the people you are meant to fellowship through the ups and downs of this life with, so that we can be "filled with the fruit of righteousness that comes through Jesus Christ—to the glory and praise of God" (Philippians 1:11, NIV).

Reflection

o   Do you have this God given gift of fellowship in your life?

o   In what ways can you intentionally seek this fellowship?

Prayer

Lord, you created me. You know my need for fellowship. You created fellowship so that our hearts could become more like you. Please forgive me for isolating myself, for not seeking out this gift. Thank you for the people in my life that you have given me. I pray that you will surround me with people who I can fellowship with in prayer and serving, accept and give grace to, and to love with a heart reflecting your fruit.

Ten

Living in The Now

What would you do today, if you knew you only had thirty days left to live? Would you live differently if your days were numbered?

There was a season of my life where my days were literally quite numbered, counting down to a day that would forever change our family, to a day where I might have to be away from them for a time. I was doing my best to memorize their faces and record their laughter and soak up every moment, whether it was tantrums or kisses.

There was a dreading of tomorrow and what would come, my chest threatened to explode and my eyes released flowing rapids in fear of my future. *There were plenty of regrets about yesterday,* the illuminating of sin and the shame that came with that, and the grieving for the way my sins affected my family. *But there was an utter need for love and joy in the moments of today.* I wanted to stop time, bottle it up, so I could savor every sweet, even every bitter, moment, so I could go back and taste the goodness, His goodness, again.

During that time, our pastor did a series at church called, "Living in The Now," and it was exactly what my heart needed, a reminder that this life is a breath, and our days are both long and short, and our time on earth should be spent in fellowship and love and serving Jesus. Days spent working and mothering and wifing come with so much exhaustion and impatience, but we are told to find joy, to find purpose in ALL of the moments we are given.

"Our days may come to seventy years, or eighty, if our strength endures; yet the best of them are but trouble and sorrow, for they quickly pass, and we fly away...Teach us to number our days that we may gain a heart of wisdom" (Psalms 90:10-12 NIV). This life is a breath in relation to the eternity that we have in Him. He has promised life eternal for those who believe in Him; whoever believes in Him has life, and whoever does not believe does not have life (1 John 5:11-12, NIV). These verses saying that we will live up to seventy years, maybe eighty if you're healthy and eat an apple a day, but so many of those years are spent in difficulty, trials, battles. If we truly lived as if our days were numbered, we would find the time and put in the effort to loving people and enjoying the moments until we fly away. And there is just no way to do that if you are worried about tomorrow or yesterday.

I have this battle inside of me on long days at home with toddlers. There is a knowing that all of the moments are fleeting; they will only be this small for so long, the sweet little "coos" will turn into "no," the tricycle will become a car, boy friends to boyfriends, the stuffed football into a leather one. And I want to enjoy every moment because it goes by so fast. The other side of this battle is the difficulty to "enjoy" waking up every two hours with a newborn, or changing a diaper that smells so bad it burns your nostrils, only to have that little one poop again the second you have the new diaper secured, or when both kids are crying at the same time, or when one is having a screeching meltdown over candy while the other cries because her cup is the wrong color.

What I have learned is that life does go fast, incredibly too fast, and in those moments, you just have to take a breath, say a prayer to Jesus, and give more of yourself, even if you feel like there's not enough left to give because those little ones rely on you. Smile because you're in the trenches of raising those babies, and one day, you will get to see and enjoy all of the hard work of these younger years, and maybe you will even miss it.

If you're not a mother, think of the moments of your work day where your patience is tested. Think of the relationships that leave you feeling drained instead of full. Think of the bills that never seem to be paid on time. Think of the tiredness that comes with the keeping of a household. How, in those moments, can you choose to find joy? How can you find Jesus and honor Him in your life?

The most important part of living in the now, is that you can't find joy in numbered days when relying on your own strength. It is only by a relationship with Jesus that you can be the wife, mother, daughter, woman, friend that you are called to be. When you rely on Him and have a relationship with Him, He gives you His grace and ability to love and serve others, which is so much more abundant than any ability you have when relying on yourself. We are flawed and sinful. Our hearts are impure and unable to love like Jesus. He is constantly perfect and forever giving of patience, kindness, and love. If you don't rely on Him, your patience with your husband, kids, or coworkers will be short. If you don't rely on Him, your kindness will be limited. If you don't rely on Him, your love will be conditional and self-serving. And Satan is there whispering lies of how you can be fulfilled, happier. We feel like we'll have time to give our lives to Jesus "one day." But in a life that is described as a morning mist, a rainy day fog that clears before mid day, in a life where tomorrow isn't promised, we have to choose today.

■ ■ ■

Satan says one day, but Jesus says today.

■ ■ ■

Choose today to show the love of Jesus. Choose today to serve the King. Choose today to let Him use you in the building of His Kingdom.

These days we're given on earth, this now that it is so imperative to find joy in, is for His glory, His Kingdom. There's a story in the Bible about Martha and her sister, Mary. Martha loved and trusted God, she had seen His miracles, but still almost missed the true purpose of our numbered days because she was just too busy. Jesus, the son of God was in her living room, but she was distracted. I would like to think that I would have sat and talked and abided in His presence, but I know I probably would have been dusting every surface and filling every plate too.

"As Jesus and his disciples were on their way, he came to a village where a woman named Martha opened her home to him. She had a sister called Mary, who sat at the Lord's feet listening to what he said. But Martha was distracted by all the preparations that had to be made. She came to him and asked, 'Lord, don't you care that my sister has left me to do the work by myself? Tell her to help me!' 'Martha, Martha,' the Lord answered, 'you are worried and upset about many things, but few things are needed—or indeed only one. Mary has chosen what is better, and it will not be taken away from her'" (Luke 10:38-42, NIV).

Jesus is saying to choose people, to choose relationship, to spend our numbered days serving and loving other people, yes, but in doing that, to not miss out on the enjoying of moments. Jesus didn't care if the food was prepared perfectly. He didn't check the closets for organization, or put on a white glove and look for dust on top of the bookshelf. He was there for them, for Mary and Martha and for you and me.

Martha was a doer; she wanted to lovingly serve Jesus; Martha was keeping the traditional role of a woman, cooking and cleaning and preparing for a guest, and she protested when Mary wasn't adhering to those norms. But in worrying about those things, she missed out on the opportunity to simply sit and listen at His feet. Mary "sat at the Lord's feet and listened to what he was saying;" she wasn't distracted; she wasn't checking her watch, and she wasn't worried about anything but the most important thing (Luke 10:39, NIV). This is the same Mary who later fearlessly pours the oil on Jesus' feet. This moment setting the foundation for her relationship with Him, a daily life choice to sit at His feet.

Jesus calmly and understandingly addresses her, "Martha, Martha," the sweetest, most personal, quiet hushing and knowing of her heart. He says, "you are worried and upset about many things, but few things are needed" (Luke 10:41, NIV). I picture Him placing his hands on her cheeks, for full attention and in the most loving way, correcting her. Because He is correcting her here. He is taking up for Mary and her decision to simply sit at His feet, the same way He did when Judas questions her pouring of the oil. Her sister was doing right according to Jesus, not only was she right, but she clearly had an understanding of Jesus' teachings that Martha just wasn't getting.

Have you ever looked around and compared what you're doing to what others are doing? Look God! I brought this family dinner, and I served at church, and I prayed extra long today! Meanwhile, looking around seeing others not even completing the things on their list, but still finding joy in every moment.

■ ■ ■

Comparison is not a healthy way to live our life of numbered days.

■ ■ ■

God knows your heart, and if you are joyfully serving Him and loving others with Him as your audience, that is wonderful. Many more of us slip into this comparison of doing, and Jesus' response to this is loving correction. He teaches Martha not to compare herself to Mary, not to worry about what Mary is doing because it's actually what is best. Instead of comparing and condemning and questioning the fairness of her work versus Mary's leisure, she should join Mary at His feet.

Martha was missing the very reason for His visit, and I imagine that was very frustrating for Martha because I identify with her so much. I feel like I know the hurt this might have caused. She was doing her best. She was entertaining and making sure He was comfortable and fed and served. But Jesus was there for time and prayer and teaching and communication, fellowship with them. We need to live with passion and energy and enthusiasm and a focus on Jesus.

When I think about how to apply this to my life, it looks something like this: the clean dishes in the dish washer can wait when the baby needs snuggles. Who cares if the load in the washer has to be cycled again when there is tea to sip at a picnic with the toddler queen? The urgent messages at work can wait when a parent asks for prayer. The vacuum will be there tomorrow, and so will the crumbs on the floor, but the coffee with a sweet friend and a listening ear when she needs it, is needed now.

Loving people and leaving a legacy by impacting them with your time, effort, and energy glorifies God and fulfills your purpose. That is the meaning of life. That is your calling; loving people and serving them in His name.

■ ■ ■

When Jesus comes, or your breath of a life is over, He isn't going to be checking the cleanliness of your home, but your heart.

■ ■ ■

Even though it might drive you crazy, you have to put down the broom, disarm yourself of the Clorox wipes, leave the dishes in the sink, and enjoy your time with family. Cultivate your relationship with Jesus, put your phone down and spend time with your husband or loved ones. These are THE most important things. Don't miss out on giggles and memories because you're standing over the sink scrubbing a dish, or miss out on precious hugs and horsey rides because you just had to wipe down the stove. Don't miss out on the goodness of Jesus or His purpose for you because the floor just had to be mopped.

Yes, the moments are fleeting. Kids grow up. Husbands get older. But the relationships forged by the love of Jesus are forever. Find joy in the little moments, glorify God while you wash the dishes because you had food to eat. Find thankfulness amidst piles of clothes to wash and fold because you love the people who wear them. Live in the now, and live in it with joy and love and the heart of a servant, so that your life can bring glory to God.

"Now listen, you who say, 'Today or tomorrow we will go to this or that city, spend a year there, carry on business and make money.' Why you do not even know what will happen tomorrow. What is your life? You are a mist that appears for a little while and then vanishes. Instead, you ought to say, 'If it is the Lord's will, we will live and do this or that.'" (James 4:13-15, NIV). James says that our life is a mist that appears and then vanishes. If you have ever driven through the mountains in the morning, you know how quickly that fog lifts. There is nothing wrong with making plans for the future, goals for the days ahead, but in making those arrangements, pray that they are God's plan for your life because the days you are given should be spent building His Kingdom.

Living in the now boils down to selflessly loving others, loving and serving God, giving Him your life to use to further His Kingdom, and that is too much for us to do on our own. Living in the now requires trust in God and His goodness. We can't do this without Him. With His grace and strength, we can do this in our numbered days because "love never fails" (1 Corinthians 13:8, NIV). And if our focus is loving God and loving others, if that is our primary motivation, we cannot fail.

So, if my days on this earth are but a fog lifting and tomorrow isn't promised, I will choose to abide in Him all of my numbered days, seeking His will, glorifying His name by loving others, and with thanksgiving in ALL circumstances because that is our purpose.

Reflection

o   Do you find it difficult to find joy in your days?

o   How can you allow Jesus to bring purpose to your numbered days?

Prayer

Jesus, your life given for me is reason to celebrate. You have given me reason to be joyful in every day, every circumstance. Because of you, I have eternal life. Forgive me for getting caught up in daily tasks, forgive me for a bitter heart, when my days should be full of joy in you. Thank you for this calling. Thank you for your goodness. Please help me to find joy in any season. Please gently remind me when I need to simply sit at your feet.

Eleven

"I am"

The first time we ever see the statement, "I am," is in the Old Testament. Moses, a shepherd, was tending the flock of his father in law. He led the sheep too far into the wilderness, and he found himself at Horeb, or the mountain of God. While he was there, an angel of the Lord appeared to him in the flames of a bush that was on fire, but wasn't burning up. "God called to him from within the bush, 'Moses! Moses!' And Moses said, 'Here I am.'" God told him to take off his sandals because he was standing on holy ground, and God said, "I am the God of your father of Isaac and the Go of Jacob." Moses hid his face because he was afraid. God tells Moses that He has heard the cries of His people and came down to rescue them from the Egyptians. God's message to Moses was clear. He told Moses to go to Pharaoh and bring His people, the Israelites, out of Egypt. Moses' response is like so many of ours would be; why me? Who am I to go to Pharaoh and deliver these people to freedom? God tells Moses that He will be with him, but Moses is still not convinced. "Suppose I go to the Israelites and say to them, 'The God of our fathers has sent me to you,' and they ask me, 'What is his name?' Then what shall I tell them?' God said to Moses, 'I AM WHO I AM. This is what you are to say to the Israelites: 'I AM has sent me to you'" (Exodus 3:1-14, NIV).

Okay, so we have Moses, who was supposed to be taking care of the sheep that weren't his own, who was trusted with a job and ended up lost in the wilderness. This is who God chose to reveal Himself to and who God chose to deliver His people from Egypt. Moses felt too unworthy to even look at the bright fire of God, let alone trusted with this task that seemed bigger than he knew his abilities to be. In the next chapter we are going to talk about who God chooses to use, but take a minute and just think about that. This substitute shepherd, wandering around lost in the darkness, sees a bush on fire, and then his life purpose is changed because God gives Him this task. Moses was questioning, wondering how this would even be possible, and he didn't even know God well enough to tell these people who sent him. In this moment, we hear for the first time an "I Am" statement.

In Hebrew the words are *"ehyeh asher ehyeh."* I did some research because I definitely don't know Hebrew, and the word *ehyeh* is the first person common singular of the verb *"to be."* If you weren't an English major and you're like, huh? Stick with me. This word, this common verb, would have been used in everyday conversations: "I am watching the sheep," "I am his mother," or "I am the owner of this house." However, when used as a description, *I AM* is a statement of presence, sufficiency, ultimate being. A full, complete, all you need kind of being. God's existence is not based on anyone or anything else. He just is. His plans are not contingent on circumstances. He promises that He is what He is, and that He will be what He will be. So this first "I am" statement is God explaining who He is; an ever constant, never changing God.

In the New Testament, Jesus gives seven "I am" statements about who he is.

I AM the bread of life (John 6:35)
I AM the light of the world (John 8:12)
I AM the gate for the sheep (John 10:7)
I AM the good shepherd (John 10:11)

I AM the resurrection and the life (John 11:25)
I AM the way and the truth and the life (John 14:6)
I AM the true vine (John 15:1)

I think Jesus adds to God's "I AM" because He knew we needed more. He knew His sheep needed more guidance from their Shepherd. We're going to break these down and see what they say about Jesus, and what they mean for us as His people. Because if we know who He is, we will know more about who we are serving, and how to be more like Him. Like Moses, we will be able to tell others who sent us.

I AM the Bread of Life (John 6:35, NIV)

We talked about this in an earlier chapter, but here, we are going to go a little more in depth about the statement that Jesus is the bread of life. We all know what bread is, right? Surely, you know that yummy, carb filled food that we crave and toast and load with butter? It's a sustaining food that, when it gets in your belly, literally expands and creates a feeling of fullness. And here Jesus says that he is the bread of life.

There are two different words for "life" that are used in the Bible; bios, or the physical breath in your lungs, and zoe, which is spiritual vitality. So, you have physical life and spiritual life and a need for each. Bios is only used 10 times; whereas zoe is used 125 times, teaching us that this zoe, this spiritual fullness is needed even more than the air we breathe. This need for a connection with our Savior is more vital to living than the filling of our lungs.

There is a type of praying, a type of seeking you may have heard of before, fasting. Fasting is when you deny yourself of the bios to seek zoe. I had never fasted before. I really really enjoy food. I couldn't imagine a day without food. I need coffee to stay awake and food to fill my belly, or I will be cranky.

But during my season of soul shattering, and in the study of this statement that Jesus is the bread of life, I felt led to give my situation, my life to God by fasting. I didn't have a set amount of time that I wanted to accomplish, just a deep need for a focus on my spiritual life, my relationship with Him. A time of recommitment and prayer about an upcoming situation.

I fed the kids breakfast that morning, all the while praying for Him to fill me up. That morning, I prayed in between diaper changes and juice refills for God to answer this prayer for my family. That morning, I prayed for God to take away any hunger pains, or use them to remind me that He alone is my provider. And before my stomach ever even pained from hunger, my phone rang. And the news I so desperately needed came. I'm not saying that fasting is a "give you whatever you want" type of prayer, but oh, how He was able to fill me when I truly realized that my zoe, my life, was His.

Jesus is the bread of life because He is the one who can provide the nourishment necessary to fill you physically and spiritually. When 5,000 people were gathered to follow and witness Jesus, the people realized they were in the middle of nowhere, a mountainside, now feeling the pains of hunger, hearing the growling from within. "When Jesus looked up and saw a great crowd coming toward him, he said to Philip, 'Where shall we buy bread for these people to eat?' He asked this only to test him, for he already had in mind what he was going to do. Philip answered him, 'It would take more than half a year's wages to buy enough bread for each one to have a bite!' Another of his disciples, Andrew, Simon Peter's brother, spoke up, 'Here is a boy with five small barley loaves and two small fish, but how far will they go among so many?'" (John 6:5-9, NIV).

God created us; He absolutely knows that we need physical filling and nourishment. So, here we have Jesus and 5,000 of his closest friends. They were right to follow, right in knowing who could fill them spiritually, but they're so quick to wonder where their food was going to come from, when the answer was sitting right amongst them. With only five loaves and two small fish, they began to worry, to question, to fear in the unknowing of how their bellies would be filled, but Jesus "already had in mind what he was going to do" (John 6:6, NIV).

And he took the bread and fish and fed everyone until they were full, and there was food left over. Let that sink in; THERE WAS FOOD LEFT OVER. In doing this, He proved that He is all that you need.

■ ■ ■

He is the provider of physical bread. He is the provider of spiritual bread. And he is all that we need to consume to feel full and nourished in this life.

■ ■ ■

Just like bread, the more you ingest and digest, the more you crave, so it is with Jesus. The more you know Him, the more you trust Him, the more you spend time in relationship with Him, the more of Him you crave. The more you are able to rely on Him as the bread of life.

I AM the light of the world (John 8:12, NIV)

In Genesis, God spoke and said, "Let there be light," and the light He created with His words was good, and it separated the darkness (Genesis 1:1-5, NIV). Before light, there was only darkness, but He decided that His creation would be bathed in light, that there was a necessary separation of light and dark. Light reveals what is hiding in darkness; light is warm; light brings growth; light shines and shows beauty; light sustains life. Think of the sun on your face as you step outside. Think of the turning on of lights in a dark house. Think of the flowers blooming in the rays of the sun. He knew His creation would need the warm embrace of the light. He knew His creation would see darkness and feel fear and need the peace that comes with illumination.

And because He created light, and He is light, comes the "I am" statement and the promise that follows: "...Whoever follows me will never walk in darkness, but will have the light of life" (John 8:12, NIV). So, not only did God create light, but a promise that anyone who follows Him will never again be surrounded and lost in the darkness. If a life with Jesus is light, then a life without Him is dark. And if we know what light is and all the goodness associated with it, the necessity of it for life and survival, why then, would we ever choose darkness? That choice in the garden, that inherited sinful nature, craves the dark because it ceases to exist in the presence of light. Jesus in us, that light in us, leaves no space left to hide.

■ ■ ■

He doesn't promise to take the darkness away, but He does promise to give us light.

■ ■ ■

The darkness is still there because no one is sinless, but we're aware of it now, able to see it in the illuminating. In darkness, is shame and guilt, but His light offers a way out of the darkness, and if Jesus is the light of the world, then, surely I want Him lighting up the dark spaces of my heart, showing me how to bring Him glory and spread His light.

I AM the gate for the sheep (John 10:7, NIV); I AM the good shepherd (John 10:11, NIV)

When I first began researching and learning what these statements mean about God, I realized there is a lot to learn about who this makes us. Because if He is the gate, and if He is the shepherd, then we are the sheep, and being a sheep doesn't really feel like a compliment. But listen to the characteristics of a sheep: they are defenseless, they tend to follow, they are stubborn, they are prone to wander, and as I hear these characteristics, I start to realize that I am like a sheep. I am weak and vulnerable and defenseless. I tend to follow other sheep in the flock, and I am definitely stubborn in my thoughts and ways and my want to control. And oh, how I have wandered in the darkness. I'm easily rattled when something causes me fear or messes with my peace.

■ ■ ■

My heart longs for the stability and peace that comes with the presence of a shepherd.

■ ■ ■

The shepherd knows all the needs of his flock, every unique need of every individual sheep, and the sheep, they know His voice. He provides for them, their basic needs of water and food, but their safety and their lives are also in his hands. We talked in an earlier chapter about how the shepherd will leave the flock to find the one lost sheep, and now we know that He is the Shepherd. His role is to meet our needs, both physical and spiritual, and we can look to Him as our provider and protector.

Not only is He the shepherd who cares for His flock of tender, easily fearful sheep, but He is the gate. Jesus says, "I am the gate; whoever enters through me will be saved. They will come in and go out, and find pasture. The thief comes to only steal and kill and destroy; I have come that they may have life, and have it to the full" (John 10:9-10, NIV).

So, in Him, we have salvation, entrance through the gate that was His body, His blood shed so that we could enter into Heaven. He says that the sheep will come and go, showing, since He knows his sheep, we would enter and exit, our faith wavering, our need to wander strong. But as the gate, He doesn't put on a lock and deny the flock the chance to wander. He remains, waiting to welcome the sheep home. And the shepherd can lead the flock toward the gate, but entry is the choice of the sheep. The enemy is waiting at the gate, seeking destruction and threatening to steal our hearts, but Jesus is there to give us life to the full. Think of what this says about Him. He is saying that in the field He will watch us, protect us, provide for us, find us in darkness and lead us back to the gate, carry us if our fear is paralyzing, and then, as the gate, we have entrance through Him into eternal life. And if that is the promise of Him as our Shepherd and Gate, then I really don't mind being the sheep.

I AM the resurrection and the life (John 11:25, NIV); ...I AM the way and the truth and the life (John 14:6, NIV)

Resurrection is the action of being resurrected; which is to be raised from the dead, and more than once in the Bible, we see Jesus' resurrection power. Not only was he resurrected after the cross, but he was able to speak life back into Lazarus. These verses describe another resurrection of the son of a widow.

"Soon afterward, Jesus went to a town called Nain, and his disciples and a large crowd went along with him. As he approached the town gate, a dead person was being carried out—the only son of his mother, and she was a widow. And a large crowd from the town was with her. When the Lord saw her, his heart went out to her and he said, 'Don't cry.' Then he went up and touched the bier they were carrying him on, and the bearers stood still. He said, 'Young man, I say to you, get up!' The dead man sat up and began to talk, and Jesus gave him back to his mother" (Luke 7: 11-15, NIV).

This broken-hearted mother, who lost her husband and now her son, and is comforted by Jesus. He feels her pain, and with the touch of His hand and His spoken words, the boy sat up, and he gave him back to his mother. Again, Jesus showed his power over the grave. His limitless ability. He is life; therefore, he can bring life to a dead body and speak life to a dead soul.

Jesus' statement that he is the way the truth and the life furthers this idea that He is the resurrection and the life. We know that through him, as the gate, He is the only way to the Father. And in this statement, we hear that He is the truth.

■ ■ ■

In Him, we have this promise that His word is truth; His promises will remain.

■ ■ ■

And even when we don't see Him working, He is.

I AM the true vine, and my Father is the gardener (John 15:1, NIV)

We planted flowers in the flowerbed in front of our house, and each day, our oldest daughter prayed for those flowers. Her five year old faith asked God to keep the flowers alive, for Him to water them, give them sun, and to let them live. I love her knowing of who to take her sweet prayers to, but part of me was a little offended by this. She knew that I was not a gardener. My thumb was and is the opposite of green. Any flowers I planted lived very short lives, so she prayed a prayer to the one she didn't even know as the Gardener.

In this, if God is the Gardener, and Jesus is the vine, then we are the branches. "He cuts off every branch in me that bears no fruit, while every branch that does bear fruit he prunes so that it will be even more fruitful. You are already clean because of the word I have spoken to you. Remain in me, as I also remain in you. No branch can bear fruit by itself; it must remain in the vine. Neither can you bear fruit unless you remain in me" (John 15:2-4, NIV). So we are sheep, and we are branches. Branches on a vine, not easy flowers to tend that stay in their beds, or even wild flowers that blow in the wind, but branches on a vine.

Vines stretch and grow, climb and creep. And branches on the vine need pruning for maximum fruition, just like we need His pruning to make us more like Him. Our leaves tend to be selfish, worried about our fruit bringing our own glory, but He picks those leaves, leaving space for fruit that is of Him to grow. Fruit reflecting a soul redeemed; selfless motives, unconditional love, joy in all circumstances.

■ ■ ■

The Master Gardener prunes our branches of deadness to make room for alive fresh fruit.

■ ■ ■

He goes on to say in those verses, that we are already clean because of Him; His life sacrificed giving us eternal freedom; we are already clean. And that if we remain in Him, He will always be with us because we cannot bear fruit without Him.

Have you ever tried to bloom on your own? It's exhausting and impossible. The branches can't physically prune and water and nurture themselves, and they can't survive without an attachment to the vine, Jesus, and the branches will never reap a full harvest of fruit without the tender care of the gardener.

The gardener cherishes the vine and branches, spending time and effort, protecting and providing and pruning to prepare maximum fruition. So, we as branches need to trust in the pruning. Abide in the care of our Gardener.

■ ■ ■

Trust His good plan for you, one of the most fruit, a branch overflowing.

■ ■ ■

Let these "I AM" statements define Jesus and define you; not your circumstances, not your broken pieces, not your time spent wandering. These are truths about who Jesus is, what He has done for us, and who we are in Him. Now you can see who you are in

Him, and how much we need Him as Bread, as Light, as the Gate, as our Shepherd, as the Resurrection, as the Way, and as the Vine. Now, you can go and tell of who sent you.

Reflection

o   What did you learn about who He is?

o   What do these statements say about you?

Prayer

Father, you are the Bread of Life. You are the Light of the World. You are the Gate and Shepherd. You are the Resurrection and the Life. You are the Way, the Truth, and the True Vine. Forgive me for forgetting who you are. Jesus, forgive me for the ways I try to fill these roles on my own. Thank you for your ability to protect and provide for me. Thank you for revealing these things about yourself. Please help me to know you, know your voice, know your guidance over my life.

Twelve

Testimony

Finally, the chapter where we get to talk about who God chooses to use, and it's the last one! I promised we would talk about it, and here it is! It is something SO exciting for me to write about because the book in your hands, the words you are reading, is my testimony. And when we listen to the promptings of God, and share the story of His goodness, He will use it to further His Kingdom. That is a promise I find so much peace in. The dark places I have been, the soul shattering seasons, the fear and unknown can be outshined and replaced with the brightness of a testimony to His saving, His redemptive power.

I want to start by talking about Jonah. If you have some time, I'd recommend that you read the four short chapters of Jonah. But I'll give you the details, so we can talk about who God chooses to use. In the first chapter of Jonah, God gives Jonah the command to go to Nineveh and preach the gospel. Nineveh was a great city, full of people and wealth, but it was a place of hopelessness. Jonah was a prophet; it was literally his job to hear the Lord and minister to the people of Israel. But this calling of travel to a new place and interruption of his comfortable life, made him question the clear calling of God.

So, when Jonah hears this command from the Lord, in fear and selfishness, he runs. He flees from the calling to bring the hope of Jesus to people who desperately needed it. When he boarded a boat in his fleeing, God sent wind and storm and unrest to the sea. The captain and crew were frenzied, scared to their bones, but Jonah slept. When the people on the boat tried to wake Jonah, he admitted that it was his running from God that caused the troubled waters. He suggested that they throw him overboard, since the storm was his fault, a consequence to his action of running from the calling he knew to be his, so they did. And even in his blatant disobeying of God, God "provided a huge fish to swallow Jonah, and Jonah was in the belly of the fish three days and three nights" (Jonah 1:17, NIV).

■ ■ ■

Even in Jonah's fleeing, God saved him.

■ ■ ■

And when we hear the story of Jonah, so many of us think of the fish or whale instead of the glory of God. But this story is of His glory because God sent that fish that gulped Jonah up. And He sent it to save Jonah from the raging sea when he could have drowned. To give him the opportunity to listen, even though he chose to run. To give him the grace to try again because redemption stories reveal our selfishness, our inability redeemed by His compassion, His ability.

Jonah's days in the belly of the fish led to cries out to his God. Faith built in the knowing of sin and the clinging to the Savior, grace in the gulp of a fish. Then, the "Lord commanded the fish, and it vomited Jonah onto dry land" (Jonah 2:10, NIV). When God asks in the third chapter of Jonah, again for him to go to Nineveh, he listens. And because of God's grace and second chance and glory in brokenness, the people of Nineveh were hopeless no more because they heard the testimony of Jonah and turned from their evil ways. An entire city brought to Jesus because of the telling of His compassion; Jonah's testimony of His goodness.

King David is one of the most known characters of the Bible. He was a young shepherd, someone who defeated giants, a strong and fearless warrior, known as a man after God's heart, but we see in 2 Samuel a different side of David. He saw a woman bathing, and instead of looking away, he looked harder. He sought her out, began an affair, and later found out that she was pregnant with his child. In his sin, he ordered the death of his mistresses' husband, writing, "Put Uriah out in front where the fighting is fiercest. Then withdraw from him so he will be struck down and die" (2 Samuel 11:15, NIV). On his command, came the death of her husband, and David married his mistress.

This man's heart characterized by a love for God now turned dark by sin. And when I think about David in this situation, I just see a sheep lost in the darkness, looking around and realizing, questioning how he got there. But God didn't give up on David, and He doesn't give up on you or on me. God sent Nathan, a prophet, to open his eyes, to bring him home. Nathan tells David a story about a rich man who had many healthy sheep and a poor man with only one sick sheep that he nursed to health. When a traveler came to town, the rich man killed and cooked the poor man's sheep for dinner. And this story made David angry, still not seeing that he was the rich man. "Then Nathan said to David, 'You are the man! This is what the Lord, the God of Israel, says: 'I anointed you king over Israel, and I delivered you from the hand of Saul. I gave your master's house to you, and your master's wives into your arms. I gave you all Israel and Judah. And if all this had been too little, I would have given you even more. Why did you despise the word of the Lord by doing what is evil in his eyes?'" (2 Samuel 12:7-9, NIV). This prophet calls David out and brings him back to God and makes him aware of his sins. God made David rich, rewarded him for his faithfulness with houses and power and land and wives, and David's return was this sin. And if all that wasn't enough, He would have gladly given more. So, why then turn to evil?

And just like there were consequences to Jonah's actions, there were consequences to David's. Just as the shepherd's hook corrects the way of the sheep with a ready prompting, so God corrects the way of His people. And the sheep might limp from the correction, but that is a reminder to always stay beside the shepherd, under his protection, in his care. David mourned his son that was taken in consequence of his affair, but God gave him another son, Solomon, and God loved him. And a son Nathan, no doubt named after the man who pointed out his sin and turned him back to the God he knew and loved.

There may be corrections when our actions don't align with God's will for us, but they are done in love to bring us back to Him, His shepherd hook reached out. Despite David's sin, God loved him, forgivingly kept him in power, gracefully allowed him another son, and this story is a testimony. A man who sinned was made new, his life given to the glory of God.

If God didn't choose sinners to further His kingdom, He wouldn't have anyone on earth to choose because we are flesh, we are sinners, but our calling is to allow our inability to glorify His ability. And then to testify to that. All throughout the Bible, God used normal, everyday people. He used prostitutes and tax collectors and the poor, and He chose these people to testify for Him. Their stories of redemption even more powerful because of the places they came from.

But I find it so sweet that God would choose to use our redemption stories for good.

■ ■ ■

There is so much peace in knowing that you are not too broken; your story is not too broken.

■ ■ ■

This man in the Bible is known as being a man after God's own heart, and he wasn't without sin.

Tell others of your faults and how He forgave you. Tell others of the belly of the fish and how He saved you. Tell others of the brokenness you found yourself in, and how He put you back together piece by piece. Listen the first time, but if you don't, know that He may lovingly correct you. He will be there with grace-full arms to welcome you back, knowingly offer a second, third, tenth chance.

It's not easy. The last thing I want is my sin and inability in the light for everyone to see. You have read the words of my broken heart. I shared with you the flames of sin that left my life in dust. But I have also testified to His ability, His overwhelming forgiveness and compassion. What I fail, God passes and surpasses any projected outcomes.

■ ■ ■

He is everything I cannot be.

■ ■ ■

And my purpose is so clear to me, the calling is so clear, and I'm not running or fleeing. I have chosen to listen. To write this book and share this story of redemption because of the faith built while I was swallowed up by the fish in the troubled waters.

Because of the brokenness sin left me in, a sheep wandering, lovingly corrected by my Shepherd. Because of what He did for me. A second chance, eternal life, and I will praise and shout thankfulness for my redemption over and over. And I will give testimony to the ways He saved me to anyone who will listen. Moms on the playground, women at church, strangers at the grocery store; I want to, despite the shame and guilt of my sin and fleeing, tell of His compassion and love and ability.

The definition of testimony is: evidence or proof provided by the existence or appearance of something. The mountains and sunset and where the ocean meets the sand are testimonies of His power and beauty. The stars in the sky testify to His magnitude, and this life that we are living on earth and the eternity we get to have in Him, are a testimony of His grace and mercy. Is your life testifying to His goodness, His existence?

This book you're holding was written because a group of women felt God's leading to organize a women's conference at a local church. It was written because, at that conference, they shared their testimonies and the power of giving your life to Jesus, allowing Him to use it for His good. This book was written because their testimony so clearly illuminated my calling to share this story. This book was written because over and over, for years, God sent me signs and whispers that I needed to put these words on paper, and I learned not to flee, but I also didn't go. This book was written because there is power in the sharing of our broken pieces made new by Jesus. And when you listen to the calling, His calling, He will exceed your expectations. He will redeem the parts of your story that you thought were wasted, and when you are obedient to His calling, you can expect huge results, supernatural results.

He uses the least. He loves the sinner. He shepherds the sheep, and I am all of those things. But with my story of redemption, my testimony, when given to Him, comes revivals of faith, masterpieces from messes, cities redeemed because of testimony shared.

I hope that you have found encouragement in our dust to

restoration story because we were at court for custody battles and dropping kids off in parking lots, but now we are eating dinner at the same table, and singing, "You are my Sunshine," together as the kids close their eyes. We were paying lawyers and arguing about holidays, and now we are planning family vacations and laughing and making new memories together. We were selling our dream home with nowhere to go, and now we are all under one roof again. We were a month away from signing divorce papers, and now we're smiling and watching our kids play together in the yard, and we're dreaming of our future again. I'm forgiven, and we're forgiven, and I'm choosing to live a life reflecting redemption. And I just want to shout with joy. In this testimony, this story of mourning over the life we had traded for a crown of beauty, in this celebration of wandered sheep brought home, I pray that you that you have seen and felt Jesus here.

Sweet friend, I cry with you in the dust your life has become. I understand the shame of sin illuminated. I fight your battles with you in fellowship. I have compassion for the ways your heart has been broken. I know the anger that comes with broken trust and empathize with the toughness of forgiveness. I stand with you in the fact that His promises for you are good! I trust Jesus with the dust of your life, just like I trust Him with mine. But most of all, *I pray this testimony has called you to a life redeemed.*

Reflection

o In what ways does your life testify to His goodness?

o What is your calling?

o   Has God ever corrected you for fleeing? How?

Prayer

Jesus, you are good. Your plan for me is good. Forgive me for forgetting. Forgive me for wandering and running and the chosen sin and darkness. Thank you for your calling on my life; thank you for the testimony you have given me, the story of your goodness and mercy. Please, Lord, help me to share it with others. I need your strength to put myself aside and let your love shine through. Help me to live a life redeemed.

Printed in the United States
By Bookmasters